THE ART OF THE PANTRY

Three babies, three books

THE ART OF THE PANTRY

SAVE TIME AND MONEY
WITH 150 DELICIOUS MEALS
USING EVERYDAY INGREDIENTS

CLAIRE THOMSON

PHOTOGRAPHY BY MIKE LUSMORE

quadrille

CONTENTS

INTRODUCTION

This book concerns my love of and respect for a well-stocked pantry. By pantry, I don't mean an enormous stately-home-sized cupboard, stacked floor to ceiling with luxury preserves and pristine packets. The pantry, cupboard, store or shelf, call it what you will (larder in the UK), epitomizes the nuts and bolts that facilitate good home cooking.

In the writing of this book, with a view to its being used relentlessly and greedily by all who have bought or borrowed it, I'm looking to encourage a pantry state of mind. Stock your given space discerningly with key ingredients and this culinary framework will help you to cook more creatively, thriftily and with greater ease. A well-stocked pantry is an empowering thing, and with it, the possibility of cooking *something* from *anything* (a hard-won skill on which I pride myself) is entirely achievable.

But life would surely be a crumply, monotonous existence for everyone if all the food you ever made came solely from the dry store. So (full disclosure), this is in fact a book of two halves, since a pantry cannot stand entirely alone if your cooking is to remain inspiring and varied. For a pantry to work at optimum, it must exist in conjunction with plenty of fresh fruit and vegetables. Meat, fish, cheese and eggs can be viewed as culinary stimuli to inspire and govern which particular pantry staple you then turn to. Easy.

The synergy of cooking well and eating well is an obvious one. The better the cook, the better the food. Lucky then that cookery is one of those activities that can never outrun itself and become obsolete; there is always something to learn, whatever the caliber of cook. Cooking well takes determination and courage. A good cook does not need extravagant ingredients or gadgetry; bells and whistles do not necessarily make for good eating. What is needed is good-quality ingredients (note: this does not equate with *expensive*) and the knowledge of how and why to use them. Take soup, for example: a good soup should always start with a soffritto. Without this cooked-down, unctuous medley of vegetables, any resulting soup will fall short. A soffritto will transform a soup, giving it robust backbone and welcome complexity. Patience is crucial in soup-making. Moreover, a canny understanding of spices and herbs to flatter and invigorate more humble ingredients—lentils, grains and legumes, for example—will boost the food you cook and costs just cents.

From my time spent cooking in restaurants, I firmly believe that aceing it in the kitchen doesn't have to be about performing flashy recipes by rote with stressful precision. The more memorable chefs and cooks I have worked alongside have displayed an innate understanding of why certain ingredients work so well together and have used them simply and elegantly. These are the people I have always strived to emulate. I will never tire of cooking and accumulating food knowledge and I will always want my ordinary everyday food to be *extraordinary* food.

The week-night supper of canned sardines with breadcrumbs, fennel seeds and chili, for spaghetti, must be as delicious as the stellar Sunday offering of pork chops cooked with rhubarb and hazelnuts.

These days we are lucky with the widespread access we have to so many different ingredients. That said, and often overheard, so-called esoteric ingredients can put people off attempting to cook a certain recipe at home in their own kitchen. While I'm grateful for supermarkets and the accessibility they promote, if you shop in any Indian, Middle Eastern and Turkish, Eastern European and Asian shops, as well as trying online merchants, you will discover an inexpensive and exhaustive array of goods. Spices, grains, pulses, fermented products, various flours, cured meats and more, it is the very regionality of these ingredients that can make them feel unique—their speciality doesn't mean that they are difficult to find. Seek them out and equip your cupboard.

The contents of your pantry represent culinary independence. Ingredients for me spark adventure, a sort of '*where in the world would I like to cook?*' attitude. Take gram flour, for example: this thrifty ingredient is a pantry staple and a favorite of mine. It can be used in traditional Indian recipes, such as pakora, in southern French, in socca, and also in Italian cooking, for farinata (pages 140–2). Knowing how this amazingly versatile flour behaves when you cook with it means that in combination with other pantry and seasonal ingredients, you can make a variety of dishes from the one core ingredient.

The magpie in me appreciates the ability to be able to bend and experiment within cooking. Granted, there are certain recipes that are inviolable and for good reason. I remain in awe of the Italian grandmother who cooked for me in Naples one summer during my early twenties. Her view on *linguine con vongole* was absolute: there was one way to make the dish, and hers was the only way; any other method or deviation from ingredients simply wasn't *linguine con vongole* (more on this later).

Cooking well in my experience is about understanding ingredients. When to pile on the flavor and when to just let two or three speak for themselves.

It goes without saying that the kitchen is the axis of my household. I love the clatter and the hubbub, the way different family members interact with the same space, the sense of anticipation as smells and cooking sounds drift in and out on a slipstream. Vegetables dominate in the food I cook; olive oil and lemons are always to hand. A piece of cheese bought for a treat or a joint of meat to roast and savor on a Sunday—these are the non-essential, sometimes luxury ingredients. Above all, my pantry is the main artery of my cooking; its contents provide a reassuring system from which I cook day in, day out.

Give me an apron, a sharp knife, a chopping board and some good ingredients, and I am happy; truly I can cook almost anything. I cook because I love it and we all need to eat.

Note on recipes: All dishes serve 4 people unless specified otherwise.

1 PASTA AND NOODLES

Pasta reaches far and wide, from the traditional, rich fresh egg doughs rolled and cut by hand in the north of Italy and beyond, to the coarse semolina pastes of southern Italy fashioned by thumb and forefinger, the 'phantom pasta' category that is gnocchi and gnudi, and the Berber-invented couscous of northern Algeria. To tether these ingredients to the pantry, I will concentrate my efforts specifically on dried pasta, the sort that you buy in packets and then try desperately to duplicate in the next shop, to enable the seamless move from one bag to the next. It's usually made from hard durum wheat, the same as used to make bread, ground down and worked with water, shaped (extruded), dried and ready for use. Dried pasta is an ingredient that is as prolific as it is eccentric in terms of the sheer number of shapes and sizes. It is a grocery essential. Dried pasta is not subordinate to fresh; it is a different ingredient.

Factory or artisan produced, when purchasing dried pasta look for 'bronze die' on the label. Bronze die pasta is superior to mass-produced Teflon-cast pasta because it is extruded through traditional bronze shapes which help to create a naturally rough, porous exterior, giving the cooked pasta an irregular surface for sauce to cling to. I find some low-cost brands turn too quickly from being still gristly to flabby and bloated with the cooking water. Cook cautiously, and err on the side of less cooking time. Ideally all pasta should be cooked with a slight resistance in the center, especially if the pasta is to finish cooking in any sauce before serving. Any residual heat will then make for pasta with perfect bite. I once worked with a very assertive chef, higher up the pecking order than me, who said he could hear when pasta was perfectly cooked. I remember laughing at him, thinking to myself how pretentious he sounded. Years later, and much less recalcitrant I suppose, I will sometimes find myself snapping a strand of spaghetti close to my ear rather than biting it to see if it is ready. It only really works with long dried pasta but, sure enough, there is a different sound to the snap of uncooked and the snap of al dente. It is a quiet, tiny snap buffered by just the right proportion of softened, cooked exterior.

The pasta shape you choose must always be governed by the ingredients or sauce you want to serve it with. Short of giving a geometry lesson on pasta shapes, an awesome collection if ever there was one, I give you here a grocery-shop quartet for daily use: spaghetti or linguine (thin and long); tagliatelle, fettuccine or pappardelle (flat and long); penne, orecchiette or conchiglie (short and shapely); and orzo, ditalini or tripolini (tiny). Understanding the different properties these three styles of dried pasta deliver will determine the ingredients you shop for and stockpile on your shelves and in your refrigerator.

Pasta bridges gastronomy in a way that not many other ingredients are capable of. From fantastically elite truffle dishes, to *cacio e pepe* (made with just pasta, Pecorino and generous helpings of freshly ground black pepper), pasta is matchless in its versatility. Or rather, nearly matchless: noodles. Empirical tattletales will have it that the Venetian Marco Polo brought pasta to Italy on his return from China in the thirteenth century. And sure enough, in his journals, grandly titled Description of the World, he writes about macaroni being eaten and enjoyed in some Italian settlements on his return. The nonchalance with which he mentions it implies that pasta consumption was not so new to Italy. Myopic and at best sequential, the myth of Marco attempts to explain how two distinct continents came to share such a similar and dominant food source. Plain and simple, the likely truth was that the Chinese and much of Asia had long been expert noodle-makers and the Mediterranean, North Africa and some of the Middle East had also been making and enjoying pasta in some form for at least a couple of centuries before Marco ever made tracks to travel east.

En masse, noodles represent an inexpensive and filling ingredient. Shopping for noodles can be an intimidating task for the uninitiated. Stand in the aisles of any Asian supermarket and you will likely face a wall of noodles, all snappily dressed in very different-looking cellophane packets. Noodles come from far and wide, with China, Taiwan, Korea, Japan and south-east Asia all having their respective noodle styles. Mostly made from rice, wheat and starches like sweet potato or mung bean, dried noodles represent a comprehensive culinary pivot for the home cook. A basic rule of thumb when choosing noodles and what to serve with them is to cook to the same cuisine as the origin of the noodle. Noodles can be enjoyed hot or cold—hot in a broth, with ramen or pho being the most widely recognized, or stir-fried, or served cold and dressed, and with raw vegetables.

Wheat noodles are similar to pasta in that they are made from ground wheat grain, with salt added to soften the proteins and bind the dough. Asian wheat noodles come in various widths and their cooking times correspond accordingly. Chinese egg noodles made with wheat flour, like egg pasta, are to my mind best eaten fresh. Likewise, fat chewy udon noodles are best made and served fresh, not dried. Nonetheless, there is more than plenty to be getting along with; dried wheat noodles are a boon for any self-respecting pantry. And, for a super-quick noodle fix, I'm all for having a few of those instant noodle packets on my shelves; just ditch the seasoning packet and add your own flavor.

Japanese buckwheat noodles (soba) are an interesting and gluten-free alternative to wheat noodles. Pure 100% buckwheat noodles have a distinctive savoury, sweet, nutty taste with a dark freckled appearance. Soba noodles are good served hot or cold. It's worth noting here that some varieties of soba noodles have wheat flour added in the noodle or to coat the noodle and are not gluten-free.

Rice noodles are different from wheat, chiefly in cooking time, and are mostly sold dried. Like wheat, though, they are also sold in a dizzying variety. Rice noodles are made on an industrial scale by soaking rice grains and grinding them into a paste to cook.

The cooked paste is kneaded, rolled flat and cut down to size. The noodles are then steamed, cooled and dried, ready for packaging. From wide and flat ribbons, to slender thin shiny sticks, to the tangle of vermicelli, dried rice noodles are an easy grocery staple. Some rice noodles need boiling for only a few minutes, while others are simply soaked in hot water to rehydrate.

Most slippery of all noodles is the starch variety, made with mung bean, corn or sweet potato. These noodles are most commonly used in stir-fries, and cold in noodle salads or Vietnamese rice rolls. They take very little cooking and maintain a glassy, chewy, almost jelly-like texture when ready. Like rice noodles, they are gluten-free. Perhaps the least accessible of the three, starch noodles are worth seeking out but can be interchangeable with any thinner rice noodle varieties.

If there exists such a thing as good pantry husbandry, while the chef in me enthuses over new ingredients, gallivanting around any new food markets and shops I come across, there is a part of me that balks at the clutter of having too many opened packets on my kitchen shelves—nothing worse than tiny amounts left in packets destined for a controversial gene pool come mealtimes. When it comes to pasta and noodle buying, far better practice is to stock a few varieties, to cook with them exhaustively, and to enjoy their different qualities before moving on and experimenting with a new style. A well-stocked kitchen needn't mean piles of expensive and esoteric ingredients (here lies waste and all sorts of culinary trouble), but crucial, necessary items that will make day-to-day cooking easier. Know what you have on your shelves and use any dried pasta and noodle packets within one month of opening, as they can become brittle, cooking unevenly, if stored for too long.

If cooking well is about fostering a balance between making fast food from scratch and crafting dishes of subtlety and sustenance, pasta and noodles support a kitchen and its cooks in a way that very few other ingredients are capable of.

PANTRY BASICS

DRIED PASTA

spaghetti or linguine (long and thin)

tagliatelle, fettuccine or pappardelle (long and flat)

penne, conchiglie or orecchiette (short and shapely)

orzo, ditalini or tripolini (tiny)

NOODLES

rice noodles

wheat noodles

mung or starch noodles

buckwheat/soba noodles

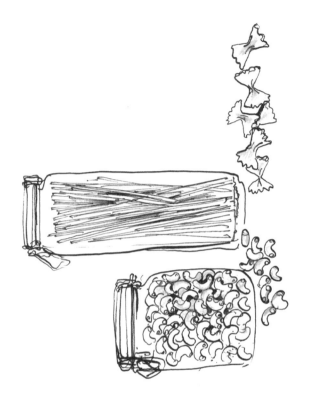

10½oz spaghetti or linguine

2¼oz/¼ cup butter

1–2 tablespoons freshly ground black pepper, or to taste (ground quite coarsely here is ideal)

4½oz/2 cups freshly grated Pecorino cheese (Romano is best—you can use Parmesan, but the result will be quite different)

Spaghetti with Pecorino and Black Pepper

Pecorino (hard ewe's milk cheese) is best to use here. You will need plenty of it, combined with the cooking water and the pepper, as this makes the sauce. Cook the pasta on the firmer side of al dente; in this and some other recipes the cooked pasta is reintroduced to the heat along with its sauce for a minute or so to meld and continue cooking in the pan. Any recipe that calls for the pasta to be drained, tossed and served immediately does not require such a lean cooking time.

Cook the pasta in salted water as per the packet instructions. Be sure to cook it on the firmer side of al dente, as you will cook it a little more in the sauce at the end.

Five minutes before the pasta is cooked, in a large saucepan over a moderate heat, melt the butter with the ground pepper to infuse the flavors.

Before draining the pasta, reserve about 3½fl oz/⅓ cup of the cooking water with a ladle (the pasta releases its starch and flavor into the cooking water).

Add the cooked drained pasta to the pan of melted butter and cook over a moderate heat for another minute. Add half the reserved cooking water and mix well. If it needs more liquid to make the sauce, add more of the remaining reserved cooking water. The consistency should be fluid but not watery.

Remove the pan from the heat. Add three-quarters of the grated cheese and mix well until the pasta is creamy and evenly coated in the resulting sauce.

Serve immediately, with the remaining grated Pecorino on top and some extra freshly ground black pepper if you like.

salt and freshly ground black
pepper

6 tablespoons extra virgin olive oil

1½oz/⅔ cup fresh breadcrumbs

2 cloves of garlic, finely chopped

1 tablespoon fennel seeds, toasted
and lightly crushed

½ teaspoon red pepper flakes,
or to taste

1 x approx. 3½oz can of sardines
(in olive oil), drained

3 tablespoons currants or raisins,
soaked in warm water and drained

3 tablespoons pine nuts, toasted

3 tablespoons capers, rinsed
and drained if salted, drained if
in vinegar

grated zest and juice of 1 lemon

10½oz spaghetti or linguine

Spaghetti with Breadcrumbs, Chilli, Fennel Seeds and Sardines

It might not sound like much, but this dish is a triumph for the pantry. Small oily fish respond well to being canned, and are largely sustainable, delicious and ridiculously good for you. Rich in omega-3 fatty acids, they give a good fishy thwack to this Sicilian-inspired pasta dish.

Put 2 tablespoons of olive oil into a small pan over a moderate heat and fry the breadcrumbs, stirring often, until crisp and golden brown. Transfer to a bowl lined with kitchen paper and set to one side.

In a saucepan heat 2 tablespoons of olive oil over a moderate heat and add the garlic, fennel seeds and red pepper flakes. Season the mix with a pinch of salt and cook for 2 minutes for the flavors to meld but without browning the garlic. Add the drained sardines, breaking them into smaller flakes and gently warming them through. Add the raisins, pine nuts, capers and lemon zest, then remove from the heat and keep warm in the pan.

Meanwhile, bring a large pot of water to the boil. Season with salt, add the pasta and cook as per the packet instructions.

When cooked, drain and stir into the sardine mixture. Add a quarter of the breadcrumbs and mix well, seasoning with salt, pepper, the lemon juice, the remaining olive oil and extra red pepper flakes if you like.

Divide the pasta between your bowls or plates, sprinkle with the remaining breadcrumbs and serve immediately.

Tagliatelle with Spinach and Hazelnuts

Use asparagus here instead of the spinach if you prefer. With so few ingredients, you want the hazelnuts to steal the show, giving a sweet nutty crunch in among the pasta ribbons.

Cook the pasta in salted, boiling water according to the packet instructions. When it is on the firmer side of al dente, remove from the heat, drain and reserve about 3½fl oz/⅓ cup of the pasta cooking water.

Meanwhile, in a separate saucepan, add the butter and garlic and melt over a moderate heat. Add the hazelnuts, parsley and half the Parmesan and season with salt and pepper.

Add the cooked drained pasta to the hazelnut pan. Stir to combine, then add the spinach, just wilting it in the hot pasta. Add a little of the reserved cooking water to loosen the pasta mix—the sauce wants to be fluid but not watery. Check the seasoning.

Divide the pasta between serving bowls and serve topped with the rest of the Parmesan.

10½oz tagliatelle, or use pappardelle or fettuccine if you prefer

salt and freshly ground black pepper

1¾oz/just under ¼ cup butter

1 clove of garlic, crushed to a paste

3½oz/¾ cup toasted skinned hazelnuts, roughly chopped

a small bunch of fresh flat-leaf parsley, leaves picked and roughly chopped

1¾–2½oz/about 1 cup freshly grated Parmesan cheese

7oz/3½ cups spinach leaves, washed, drained and cut into ribbons, or use baby spinach leaves

Pappardelle with Cream, Radicchio and Prosciutto

Beautiful to look at, flushed with pink and red, all creamy white, this particular pasta dish is all about balance. Salty (ham), bitter (radicchio) and sweet (cream), it is always a pleasure to make and eat.

1¾oz/just under ¼ cup butter

1 small onion, finely chopped

½ a radicchio, finely shredded

3½oz prosciutto, sliced into ¼–½-inch ribbons

2½fl oz/⅓ cup heavy cream

salt and freshly ground black pepper

nutmeg, freshly grated to taste, about ⅛ is ideal

10½oz pappardelle, fettuccine or tagliatelle

1¾–2½oz/about 1 cup freshly grated Parmesan cheese

Bring a large pot of salted water to the boil.

Heat the butter in a large pan over a moderate heat and cook the onion until it is soft and translucent, about 8–10 minutes. Stir in the radicchio and the prosciutto and cook for 1–2 minutes, enough for the radicchio to wilt.

Add the cream and season with salt, pepper and nutmeg to taste.

Cook the pasta as per the instructions on the packet, and drain.

Toss the cooked pasta in the cream sauce for a minute over the heat for the flavors to meld. Serve immediately, with the grated cheese.

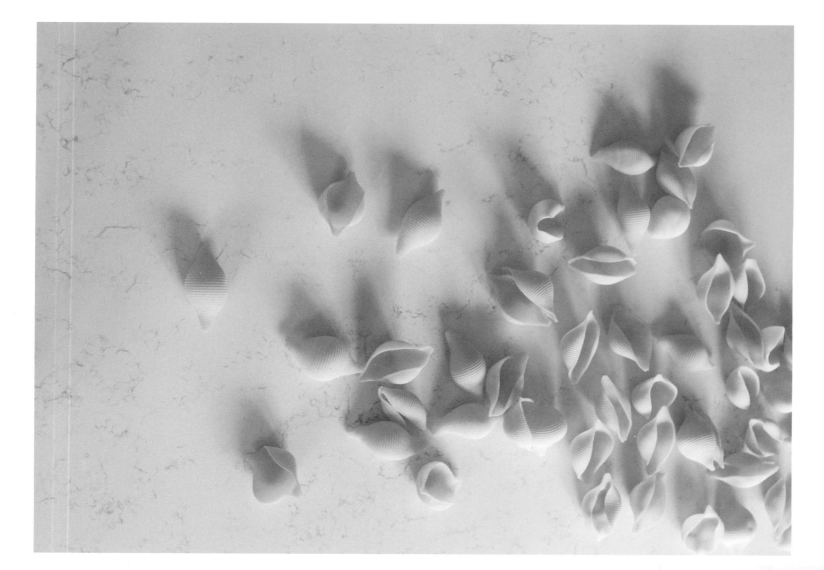

Dried Porcini with Tomato, Garlic and Clams

I overdosed on porcini when I first started cooking in restaurants, and remember making lots of flavored butters and endless vegetarian and vegan dishes with it. It wasn't long before I got sick of the sight, or at least, the earthy smell of it. Languishing in my bad books for almost a decade now, it is, however, a rightful member of the pantry. Used judiciously, porcini can give flavor like no other. Diced zucchini added with the garlic and red pepper flakes makes for a nice variation.

1oz/about 1 cup dried porcini mushrooms

4 tablespoons olive oil

3 cloves of garlic, finely chopped

½ teaspoon red pepper flakes, or to taste

4 ripe red tomatoes, diced, or use 4 canned, drained and chopped

about 40 fresh clams, cleaned (you can use canned here if you like)

9fl oz/1 cup dry white wine

a small bunch of fresh flat-leaf parsley, leaves roughly chopped

salt

10½oz linguine, spaghetti or short and shapely pasta—conchiglie or orecchiette would be fabulous

Soak the mushrooms for about 30 minutes in enough warm water to rehydrate. Drain and coarsely chop.

Heat the oil in a medium saucepan over a moderate heat. Stir in the mushrooms, garlic and red pepper flakes and cook for 2 minutes, or until the garlic is aromatic but not brown.

Add the tomatoes and cook over a moderate heat for 5–8 minutes, until thick and rich.

Stir in the clams and the white wine, then put a lid on the pan and turn up the heat. Cook until the clams open up. As they open, remove them to a waiting bowl so as not to overcook them. Continue until all the clams have cooked and have released their juices into the tomato sauce. Discard any that refuse to open.

With the clams all cooked and reserved on a plate, reduce the tomato and mushroom mix until slightly thickened, about 6–8 minutes, and stir in the chopped parsley.

Cook the pasta in salted boiling water until al dente, as per the packet instructions, and drain, reserving a little of the pasta cooking water in case you need it to loosen the sauce. Add the cooked pasta to the tomato and porcini sauce, adding a spoonful or so of the cooking liquid if necessary.

Reunite the cooked clams with the pasta in the pot and serve immediately.

olive oil, to cook and dress the pasta

4oz guanciale or pancetta, cut in ¼-inch slices, then cut across into thin strips

½–1 teaspoon red pepper flakes, to taste

1 small onion, finely diced

2 cloves of garlic, thinly sliced

1 x 14oz can of whole plum tomatoes, drained (keep the juice for something else)

salt and freshly ground black pepper

10½oz rigatoni or other short pasta

3oz/1 cup grated Pecorino Romano cheese (or Parmesan), to serve

All'Amatriciana

This collision of salty, spicy and sweet with pasta as catalyst originates in Rome. The trick is in managing the flavors to make an intense sauce that just coats the pasta. It wants to be not too liquid, not too dry. Guanciale is the cured jowl or cheek of pork; the fat renders in a different way from bacon and pancetta, almost melting, not so much crisping, as you cook it. If you can't get hold of it, a piece of bacon you can cut to size or some pancetta will do well enough.

Heat about 1–2 teaspoons of olive oil in a pan over a medium heat. Add the guanciale and cook until golden, about 4 minutes. Add the red pepper flakes and stir well, then add the onion and garlic and cook, stirring often, until soft, about 8–10 minutes. Add the tomatoes, mashing them down with a wooden spoon. Reduce the heat to low, and cook, stirring occasionally, until the sauce thickens, about 15–20 minutes.

Meanwhile, bring a large pot of water to the boil. Season with salt, add the pasta and cook as per the packet instructions. Drain, reserving about 3½fl oz/⅓ cup of the pasta cooking water.

Add the drained pasta to the sauce and toss together vigorously to coat. If the sauce is too thick (you want it to cling, just coloring the pasta, but not be swamped), add some of the reserved pasta.

Stir in half the grated cheese and transfer the pasta to bowls, dividing the remaining cheese per bowlful.

Roasted Tomato and Oregano Timbale with Yogurt Topping

A baked dish with a crust is a simple definition of a timbale. Using a high-sided cake tin with a removable bottom will give it a spectacular circumference when you come to serve it. The yogurt coagulates with the cornstarch and halloumi here, baking beautifully—all creamy and blistered—hiding the layers beneath, and the flavors prompting thoughts of Greece.

Preheat the oven to 400°F/gas mark 6.

Line a baking sheet with baking parchment, brushed with 2 tablespoons of the olive oil.

Cut the eggplant into ½-inch thick slices and lay them on the prepared baking sheet. Season with a little salt. Bake for about 12–15 minutes, until soft and bronzed.

Likewise, place the tomatoes in a single layer on another baking sheet and drizzle with 1 tablespoon of olive oil, a pinch of salt and 1 teaspoon of oregano. Bake until soft and cooked through, about 10 minutes.

Cook the pasta as per the packet instructions, keeping it firmly al dente. Drain.

Meanwhile, in a separate saucepan over a moderate heat, fry the onion in 2 tablespoons of olive oil for about 8–10 minutes, until soft and translucent. Add the garlic and cook for 1 minute more, until fragrant. Add 2 teaspoons of oregano, the drained canned tomatoes, a big pinch of salt and some black pepper to taste. Mash the tomatoes down with a spoon and continue to cook for about 8–10 minutes for the flavors to meld. With the tomatoes ready, add the cooked pasta and a spoonful of olive oil, stirring well to coat.

CONTINUED

FOR THE PASTA
5 tablespoons olive oil

1 large eggplant

salt and freshly ground black pepper

30 or so cherry tomatoes, or 8 large tomatoes cut in half

4 teaspoons dried oregano

10½oz macaroni, ziti, rigatoni or penne

1 onion, finely chopped

2–3 cloves of garlic, chopped small or crushed

1 x 14oz can of tomatoes, drained (keep the juice for another time)

FOR THE TIMBALE TOPPING
1lb 2oz/2¼ cups Greek yogurt

2 medium eggs, beaten

3½oz/about 2 cups coarsely grated halloumi cheese, or use Parmesan

1 tablespoon cornstarch

¼ of a nutmeg, freshly grated

salt and freshly ground black pepper

Meanwhile make the yogurt topping by whisking the yogurt with the eggs, grated cheese and cornstarch in a bowl. Season with the nutmeg and plenty of freshly ground pepper.

Grease an 8-inch cake tin with a removable base with a little butter or olive oil. Layer some of the pasta on the bottom. Add a layer of the roasted tomatoes and eggplant. Add a couple of tablespoons of the yogurt mix, dribbled over the tomatoes and eggplant, then add another layer of the pasta, another layer of the tomatoes and eggplant and a final layer of the pasta.

Finally, top with the remaining yogurt sauce, spreading it out equally, with an additional drizzle of olive oil and the remaining oregano.

Bake in the oven for 20–30 minutes, until the yogurt top is golden and firm to touch. Remove from the oven and let the timbale rest for 5–10 minutes, then remove from the tin and serve.

Lentils and Tiny Pasta

Lentils and tiny pasta served together, loosened with a little of the cooking water (not a soup, not a stew and certainly not a pasta salad), topped with a blizzard of grated Parmesan, is my pantry staple supper all year round. Cooked down with carrots, celery and garlic, lentils are anything but humble. You could add some diced bacon to the vegetables as they cook, but I rarely bother. Use green or brown lentils for an earthy, peppery bite; red lentils won't work as well here.

3 tablespoons olive oil, plus extra to serve

2 bay leaves

1 onion, finely diced

2 carrots, peeled and finely diced

2 celery stalks, finely diced

3 cloves of garlic, finely chopped

a few sprigs of fresh thyme, sage or rosemary, leaves finely chopped

9oz/1¼ cups green or brown lentils

9oz tiny pasta—stellette, ditalini, tripolini . . . .

approx. 3oz/1 cup freshly grated Parmesan cheese

a small bunch of fresh flat-leaf parsley, leaves roughly chopped

Heat 2 tablespoons of olive oil in a large pan, then add the bay leaves, onion, carrots and celery and cook for 8–10 minutes, until very, very soft. Add the garlic and cook for 1 more minute, until fragrant, then add the hard herbs.

Add the lentils and stir until they are coated with the oil and vegetables, then add 1⅓ pints/3 cups of cold water and cook for about 20 minutes, or until the lentils have softened. Keep an eye on the pan and top up with a little boiling water if necessary.

Cook the pasta in salted boiling water as per the instructions on the packet. Drain, reserving about 3½fl oz/⅓ cup of the cooking water.

Combine the lentils with the cooked pasta, loosening with some of the reserved pasta water if necessary, and add half the cheese, mixing well to combine.

Add the chopped parsley to the pasta and lentils and mix.

Divide the pasta and lentils between bowls and serve with the remaining cheese and an extra drizzle of olive oil if you like.

Quick Fix Miso Ramen

Absolutely do have some instant noodles in your kitchen. Super-cheap and super-quick, they are a valuable pantry ingredient. Here in this quick-fix ramen, don't bother using the little sachet (eerily potent for something so tiny!) that accompanies the noodles; flavor, nutrients too, can come from elsewhere.

Miso should be a staple of any pantry. Used in Japan as a general seasoning, it is made from fermented soybeans, salt and a friendly natural fungus. Specialist misos can have other ingredients added during the ferment, such as rice, buckwheat and barley. Dark miso is fermented for longer and has a more intense taste, while light miso is pale with a sweeter taste. Most supermarkets will stock a basic miso paste, and it is a very handy ingredient to have in your refrigerator. With characteristic flavors of salty, sweet, earthy, fruity and savory, miso is most commonly served as a soup when mixed with dashi (kelp and preserved tuna) stock. Miso can also be used as a dressing for many Asian-inspired salads or as a marinade. Kept in the refrigerator, miso has a long shelf life, up to a year at least.

Like miso, mirin is also worth shelf space. A sweet Japanese wine, mirin lends mild acidity to many dishes. Buy some. If you don't have any mirin, but need to ape the sweet tangy liquid, you can use sherry or Marsala or some rice vinegar mixed with a little brown sugar to taste.

4 packets (individual portions) of instant noodles

1¾ pints/4 cups chicken or vegetable stock (or boiling water mixed with some bouillon powder)

1 teaspoon gochujang (Korean red pepper paste)

2 heaped tablespoons miso paste (dark or light, as you like)

2 tablespoons mirin

1 tablespoon sesame oil

2 cloves of garlic, finely chopped

¾ inch fresh ginger, finely chopped

Remove the noodles from the packet. Don't bother with the flavoring sachet.

Bring the stock to the boil in a saucepan. Add the gochujang, miso, mirin, sesame oil, garlic and ginger. Add the noodles and remove from the heat. Leave to sit for a minute or two to soften.

Divide the noodles between your bowls, topping each up with the broth and adding any garnishes.

GARNISHES

Choose from the following, to add texture to the finished noodles:

- vegetables: shredded cabbage, thin sticks of carrot, radish or daikon, spinach or chard leaves cut into ribbons, sliced mushrooms, thinly sliced shallot or red onion, sliced green onions, beansprouts, cooked broccoli, fresh or frozen peas, edamame, frozen (defrosted) spinach, shredded lettuce, sweetcorn, cooked green beans, sliced cooked zucchini or cooked eggplant

- eggs: fried eggs, sliced hard-boiled eggs, sliced pickled eggs, poached eggs, beaten raw egg (added to the hot stock and noodles, ribboning the egg through the liquid to form small separate threads)

- meat: cold leftover roast meats, sliced cured ham, cooked bacon, cooked sausage or meatballs, sliced frankfurters

- tofu: diced cold tofu or fried tofu

- chili oil: add extra per bowlful (see page 168)

- sesame seeds: toasted

- lime: wedges

- herbs: basil, cilantro

Khao Soi Noodles

Thai curry pastes add a pungent boost to many dishes. You can make your own, but there are some brilliant versions available to buy fresh or with a longer shelf life. The trick to getting the most out of them is to almost fry the paste along with the garlic, unlocking the flavor, before you begin adding any other ingredients. Use wide flat rice noodles here in this fragrant spicy broth.

2fl oz/just under ¼ cup vegetable oil

4 cloves of garlic, finely sliced

3 tablespoons Thai red curry paste—use more if you like it spicy (or less!)

1 tablespoon curry powder

1 teaspoon ground turmeric

4 boneless skinless chicken pieces (thigh is best), thinly sliced (equally, cold leftover roast chicken or pork here will work well enough)

7fl oz/just under 1 cup chicken stock

1 x 14oz can of coconut milk

1 tablespoon fish sauce

1 tablespoon brown sugar

7oz rice noodles

Put the oil into a medium saucepan over a moderate heat and cook the garlic for about 30 seconds.

Add the curry paste and the spices and cook for another 30 seconds, giving everything a good stir.

Add the chicken and stir to coat in the sauce. Add the chicken stock, coconut milk, fish sauce and finally the sugar. Bring to the boil, then lower the heat and simmer uncovered for about 30 minutes. Taste and adjust the seasoning, remembering that the fish sauce should make the sauce salty enough.

Cook the noodles according to the packet directions, then drain and divide them between the bowls. Top with the sauce and serve immediately with the garnishes.

GARNISHES

Choose any or all of the below; you want to add texture to the finished noodles:

- thinly sliced raw shallot or red onion
- sliced green onion
- beansprouts
- Thai basil leaves
- cilantro leaves, roughly chopped
- mint leaves, roughly chopped
- peanuts or cashew nuts, roughly chopped
- limes, cut into wedges
- red pepper flakes

Ginger Soba Noodles

Best served icy cold, with the buckwheat noodles soaking up the gingery lime and sesame dressing. Any leftover cold roast chicken, beef or pork would be terrific here, or tofu too, but mostly I make this as is. Especially good in a lunchbox, stored in the refrigerator.

7oz soba noodles

1 tablespoon groundnut, sunflower or vegetable oil

juice of 1 large lime (or 2 small)

3 tablespoons sesame oil

1 tablespoon soy sauce

½ teaspoon brown sugar

¾ inch fresh ginger, grated

3 tablespoons sesame seeds

3 or 4 green onions, finely sliced

ice cube, per serving (optional)

Cook the noodles as per the packet instructions. Drain, then cool under a running tap. Drain again, and douse with the groundnut oil to prevent them from clumping together.

In a bowl, mix the lime juice, sesame oil, soy sauce, sugar and ginger.

Toast the sesame seeds in a dry frying pan over a moderate heat until golden.

Add the dressing to the cold noodles and mix well.

Serve the noodles with the spring onions and sesame seeds scattered over the top. Pop on an ice cube, if liked, for extra coldness.

Firecracker Noodles

'Firecracker' because these noodles explode with flavor when you eat them. With a deep, spicy, sweet heat and good contrasting textures, there's nothing subtle about this dish. Sichuan peppercorns are an intriguing and fabulous ingredient—search them out in any Asian supermarket or online.

2–3 teaspoons sesame oil

1 teaspoon soy sauce

1 teaspoon ground Sichuan pepper (use equal amount of black pepper here if you prefer)

5½oz chicken, beef or pork fillet, thinly sliced

7oz wheat noodles

vegetable oil, for cooking

1 large shallot, finely sliced (use an onion if you prefer)

2 large carrots, peeled and very thinly sliced

5 cloves of garlic, finely chopped

¾ inch fresh ginger, finely chopped or grated

2 bok choy, shredded

2¾oz/¾ cup peanuts, roughly chopped

1 bunch of green onions, finely sliced

FOR THE STIR-FRY SAUCE

2 tablespoons gochujang (Korean red pepper paste), or use Chinese chili bean paste

1 tablespoon soy sauce

2 tablespoons peanut butter —or use tahini here if you like

1 tablespoon honey or sugar

1 tablespoon sesame oil

½ teaspoon red pepper flakes

In a small bowl, mix together 1 teaspoon of sesame oil and the soy sauce and add the Sichuan pepper. Add the sliced meat and toss evenly to coat. Set aside and allow to marinate (an hour or so would be good).

Cook the noodles as per the packet instructions, then drain and cool under running water. Toss in a teaspoon or two of sesame oil.

In a small bowl mix the stir-fry sauce ingredients together and set aside.

Have all your stir-fry ingredients prepared and ready beside you when you begin.

Over a high heat, with a little oil in a wok or large frying pan, sear the meat until it's browned on the outside and just cooked through. Remove and set aside on a plate.

Return the wok to the heat, add a little more cooking oil and fry the shallot until soft and translucent. Add the garlic and ginger and cook until fragrant for about 30 seconds more. Add the carrots and bok choy to the wok and fry until slightly wilted. Remove and set aside with the cooked meat.

Wipe out the wok and return to the heat. Add 1 tablespoon of oil together with the stir-fry sauce. Allow this to simmer until thick and bubbly, for about 30 seconds. Add the noodles and toss until evenly coated and warmed through.

Add the cooked meat and vegetables and evenly toss over a high heat. Add half the crushed peanuts, tossing the ingredients together in the wok once again. Check the seasoning and remove from the heat.

Serve immediately, topping each bowl with the remaining peanuts and the sliced green onion.

2 PULSES

Bold cooks are those who relish the most humble ingredients. Whether you soak dried and cook fresh or simply open a can, pulses are among some of the best ingredients in the pantry. Ripe edible seeds of legume plants, harvested and dried, there are hundreds of different varieties grown around the world. Most recognizable on our shelves are dried beans, lentils and peas. Implicitly frugal, readily available, rich in protein, fiber, vitamins and minerals, pulses are tremendously valuable in the kitchen. They are also one of the most sustainable methods of food production, with one of the lowest carbon footprints in agriculture; they require less water to farm and also release nitrates into the soil to act as a natural fertilizer. A necessary crop for now and certainly for the future, pulses can be cultivated in parts of the world where drought and soaring temperatures make farming such a challenge.

In India, Pakistan, the Middle East, North Africa, South America and Europe, pulses have long been considered a key ingredient to store and use throughout the year. In Europe especially, the fava bean has been one of the most crucial, in use since the Bronze Age. Interesting, then, that nowadays fresh fava beans, picked immature and eaten seasonally, have usurped the smaller dried fava as the bean of choice. Stigmatized as a food of the poor, dried pulses fell out of favor when meat and dairy gained in popularity as the more exclusive source of protein for the wealthy. Unfortunately for pulses, their penurious reputation has proved an onerous one to shake off. Efficient to grow and brilliant to eat, we need to reclaim our pulse-eating mojo and make them a mainstay once more. Michael Pollan's rallying call of 'Eat food. Not too much. And mostly plants.' is dazzling in its sentiment and succinctness. It is the catchphrase of our generation and, fingers crossed, its efficacy has been potent. Pulse production is on the increase. Certainly one of the world's most proficient plants, there are now over 173 countries growing and exporting some 60 million metric tons of pulses a year (see www.pulses.org) and 2016 was the United Nations international year of the pulse, intended to raise the profile of pulses in the global diet.

When cooking with pulses, my approach is twofold. For quick, speedy cooking, canned beans, dried lentils and split peas fall into the category of quick-cook pulses. Ready-cooked and in the can, garbanzo and other beans, rinsed of their briny gloop, enjoy frequent use. Softer, more slippery in texture, canned beans are terrific used whole in wet, soupy dishes or mashed down with more flavor: onions, garlic, herbs and spices. The rescue ingredient for many a lunch or supper, canned garbanzo and other beans, pudgy and fulsome and taking minutes to make good, are full of sustenance and flavor. Unashamedly in cans and always on my shelves are butter beans, cannellini beans, haricot beans, kidney beans and garbanzo beans.

As for lentils, they will always be my favorite. With no need to soak and a relatively short cooking time, I see no need for the canned sort and would always cook fresh from dried. In Italy lentils indicate luck and prosperity. I like the thought that good luck is something to consume, easy to come by, convivial to share. For me, the unpretentious lentil represents the warp and weft of what it is to cook inspiring and delicious food—using ingredients, weaving them together to give form and color to the fabric of a dish. There is a dizzying assortment of lentils available. From slate gray, to red, to green and brown to coral pink, some heirloom varieties fetch a weighty price. Size, color and cost aside for me, the distinguishing feature of any lentil is how these tiny things cook in contact with liquid. Red lentils are widely available as a split lentil and share a similar affinity with split yellow peas. Both varieties cook quickly, collapsing into any ingredients you prepare them with. In haleem (see page 50), the red lentils and the split peas slump modestly among the brown rice and cracked wheat to give a mixed grain dhal with a sublime texture. Super-cheap and stocked almost everywhere, these are the indispensable handfuls to chuck into soups and purées and to cook into dhal dishes. Like porridge, not too soupy, not too starchy, these lentils respond well to assertive flavoring: turmeric to brighten, ginger to warm and spices to invigorate.

Brown lentils are widely available. Cooked considerately, these lentils taste great, will hold their shape and are easy to come by. Be warned, though, as brown lentils can cook to a mush very quickly if forgotten about. Best of all are green lentils; I like the way they hold their shape and have an earthy, peppery bite. Most supermarkets now also stock French green lentils. These lentils are a notch up from regular green and brown but not quite up there with the mottled beauty of Puy lentils, grown in the specialist Auvergne district in central France. Castelluccio lentils from Umbria in Italy, khaki in color and tiny in size, are equally exquisite.

In winter time my use of lentils will rely on a tiny dice of onions, carrots and celery, some bay leaves too, cooked down until sticky and aromatic—patience—the lentils are added and simmered in water until soft but still holding their shape. This is a dish I could eat for ever. Make enough; serve with sausages or a fried egg for supper and serve again the next day, the day after, as sauce to some pasta (see page 31). In summertime, green lentils respond brilliantly to being dressed while still warm, a salad of sorts, drunk on olive oil and good vinegar or citrus juice and given a showy burst of chopped herbs and olives (see page 52). Whatever the season and however I am cooking with lentils, I don't think I could ever be friends with someone who said they didn't like to eat them. Like tiny pebbles, dainty little things packed full of flavor, cooked lentils also age gracefully, tasting better for a day or two wallowing in a little of their own cooking liquid.

Slow-cook pulses are dried garbanzo and other beans, and all require soaking in water before using them. Plump and glistening, only after soaking can any real cooking begin. Cooked fresh, these pulses have a superior texture to their canned versions and are a brilliant substitute for grains, pasta or noodles and potatoes in everyday cooking. When you do cook with dried pulses, I think it's absolutely worth cooking more than just the one meal's worth and using them incrementally over a few days, throwing them into soups, stews, warm salads, on to toast, into frittatas or blitzing them into a purée. You know the drill: tahini, garlic, lemon juice, water and salt drowned in olive oil for hummus. Better still, and because I'm a tiny bit bored of the beige stuff, white beans (cannellini preferably) freshly cooked and blended with some of the bean cooking liquor, some garlic and salt, barely warm and bathed in a fruity olive oil. On toast, with bread, this is a great dish, so very simple. And while the UK and US may have cut their culinary ties (give it time . . .) with dried fava as the common use for bean crops, you can still buy the dried beans from many Mediterranean grocery shops and online stockists. Prepare these fudgy beans like they do in Egypt, cooked down with onions, cumin and plenty of fresh herbs as ful medames (see page 64). Commonly eaten at breakfast (and also to break the fast), it is stuffed in pita bread with chopped salad, hard-boiled egg and lemon wedges. Alternatively, buy split dried fava beans to soak and blitz raw for the falafel recipe (see page 66). With a crisp shell and a vivid green interior, these falafel are knockout. Any stodgy orbs masquerading as falafel will be put to shame.

As with most things left sitting on a shelf, time will eventually hamper quality. Although dried, it is best to check the production date on any packets of dried pulses you buy. Try to buy from the last season's harvest if you can. These pulses will rehydrate more evenly and cook more quickly. The older the pulse, the drier the texture. Flavor will also deteriorate. Try to buy pulses from shops with a high turnover—this way you'll know the pulses are likely to be fresher. May the pulse be with you.

PANTRY BASICS

QUICK PULSES (CANS)

haricot beans

cannellini beans

red kidney beans

butter beans

garbanzo beans

black turtle beans

QUICK PULSES (DRIED)

split peas

red lentils

green and brown lentils

SLOW PULSES (DRIED)

cannellini beans

fava beans

borlotti beans

garbanzo beans

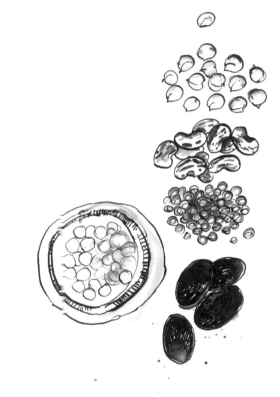

QUICK PULSES

Haleem—but without the meat

Commonly served in India, Pakistan, central Asia and the Middle East, haleem, to use just one of its names, is a multi-pulse and grain dhal, and there are many versions of it. My version uses lentils, barley, cracked wheat and also meat, but I've excluded meat (lamb or mutton) because I like it well enough without—it makes for a brilliantly thrifty and flavor-packed mid-week supper. A tarka is a spiced oil preparation and can be added at the beginning and also at the end of a dish.

1¾oz/¼ cup red lentils

1¾oz/¼ cup split peas

1¾oz/¼ cup cracked wheat or barley

2½oz/¾ cup brown rice

2 tablespoons vegetable oil

1 cinnamon stick

1 teaspoon cumin seeds

2 bay leaves

1 onion, finely diced

1 carrot, peeled and grated

1 teaspoon grated ginger

3 cloves of garlic, finely chopped or crushed

3 whole canned tomatoes, drained of juice and roughly chopped

1 teaspoon ground turmeric

2 teaspoons garam masala

¼–½ teaspoon red pepper flakes (more if you like spice)

1 teaspoon ground cumin, toasted

1 teaspoon salt

freshly ground black pepper

1¾oz/about ⅓ cup frozen peas or cooked chopped green beans

lime wedges, to serve

Soak the lentils, split peas, cracked wheat and brown rice together in cold water for about 1 hour.

Heat the oil in a saucepan over a moderate heat. Add the cinnamon stick, whole cumin seeds and bay leaves and fry for 1 minute. Add the onion and carrot and cook until soft, about 10 minutes, then add the ginger and garlic and cook for 1 more minute.

Add the chopped tomatoes and the ground spices and simmer for a minute, until the tomato is softened.

Add the drained lentils, split peas, cracked wheat and brown rice. Mix well and add the salt and plenty of freshly ground black pepper.

Add 8fl oz/just under 1 cup of cold water and bring to the boil. Skim off any froth that surfaces and reduce the heat to a simmer.

Cook for 30–40 minutes, until the brown rice is cooked through. The lentils, split peas and cracked wheat will cook before the brown rice. Add the frozen peas or beans towards the last 5 minutes of cooking time.

FOR THE TARKA
2 tablespoons cooking oil

1 tablespoon mustard seeds

1 fresh green chili, finely sliced

a pinch of ground turmeric

a small bunch of fresh cilantro, stalks finely chopped and leaves roughly chopped

Meanwhile make the tarka to finish the haleem. Put the oil into a small frying pan over a high heat. When it is just about to begin smoking, add the mustard seeds and green chili. The seeds will pop and crackle. Fry for 30 seconds, then remove from the heat and add the turmeric and cilantro stalks.

Serve the haleem with the tarka poured over, the chopped cilantro leaves and some wedges of lime.

14oz/2½ cups green or brown lentils

1 teaspoon salt

½ tablespoon red wine vinegar

grated zest and juice of 1 orange

4–5 tablespoons olive oil

a small bunch of celery leaves, roughly chopped (use any pale stalks, finely chopped)

a large bunch of fresh mint, leaves roughly chopped

2¼oz/½ cup green olives, pitted and roughly chopped

freshly ground black pepper

Lentils with Green Olives, Celery Leaf, Mint and Orange

Serve these lentils with grilled mackerel, canned fish, roast chicken or lamb, or mozzarella. They also make brilliant leftovers to shower over salads and pile on toast.

Rinse the lentils in cold water, then put them into a saucepan and cover with 1¾ pints/4 cups of cold water.

Bring to the boil, skimming off any froth that surfaces.

Simmer for 20–30 minutes, until the lentils are cooked through but still with slight resistance. Add the salt 5 minutes before the end of the cooking time.

Drain the lentils and put them into a bowl.

Dress the lentils while still warm with the red wine vinegar and the orange juice. Add the orange zest and olive oil.

Add the celery leaves and mint and the chopped olives. Mix well and taste for seasoning. Serve just warm.

Red Lentils—a hummus
of sorts

Red lentils, super-cheap and easy to come by. Blended, they make for a fast, whippy hummus here.

9oz/1½ cups red lentils, rinsed and drained

2 cloves of garlic, peeled and halved

juice of 1 lemon

5½oz/¾ cup tahini

1 tablespoon baharat blend 2 (see page 164) or ras el hanout, or use equivalent measure of ground cumin and coriander, toasted

1 teaspoon salt, or to taste

extra virgin olive oil, to serve

Rinse the red lentils well and place in a saucepan with 16fl oz/2 cups of water. Over a moderate heat, bring to the boil, skimming off any froth that surfaces, then reduce the heat and simmer until tender, about 15 minutes. Drain and cool.

Put the cooked lentils and the garlic into a food processor and blend for a minute until smooth.

Add the lemon juice, tahini, spices and salt, and blend again for another minute. By eye, add between 3 and 5 tablespoons of cold water to the mix, processing until the hummus is smooth, aerated and creamy.

Taste, then adjust the seasoning, adding more lemon juice or salt, if required.

Serve the hummus on a plate, swamped with a good measure of olive oil.

Bean Chili with Cinnamon and Bay

Canned beans made ballsy. I've given two additional variations here: baked under a blanket of cornbread, or roasted in bell peppers with cheese and sour cream. Be bold with the chili and generous with the chopped salad, all spiky with lime juice and seasoned with salt.

Put the oil into a heavy-bottomed frying pan over a moderate heat and fry the cinnamon, bay leaves, celery, green bell pepper and onion until the vegetables are soft, about 8–10 minutes. Add the garlic and ground spices and fry for another couple of minutes.

Add the canned tomatoes and simmer for about 10 minutes.

Add the drained beans, mixing thoroughly. Add the chili paste or red pepper flakes, if using, and season with salt, then cook over a moderate heat for 5 minutes for the beans to heat up and the flavors to meld, checking the seasoning.

Take the pan off the heat and add the cilantro, then mix well and set to one side.

2 tablespoons vegetable, sunflower, or olive oil

1 cinnamon stick

2 bay leaves

2 celery stalks, finely diced

1 green bell pepper, deseeded and finely chopped

1 large onion, finely diced

2 or 3 cloves of garlic, finely sliced

1 teaspoon smoked paprika—hot or sweet, depending on taste

1 teaspoon cumin seeds, toasted and ground

1 x 14oz can of tomatoes

3 x 14oz cans of assorted beans, rinsed and drained

chipotle chili paste (optional and to taste, or use red pepper flakes)

salt

a small bunch of fresh cilantro leaves roughly chopped

FOR THE CHOPPED SALAD
avocado, diced small

ripe tomatoes, diced small

red onion, finely sliced or diced

salt and freshly squeezed lime juice, to taste

TO SERVE
sour cream

chilli sauce (see page 169)

Baked under Cornbread

Use the cornbread recipe on page 152, omitting the honey and oregano. Use the bean recipe on the previous page, hot or cold, freshly made or from the refrigerator—either is fine to bake under the cornbread.

Preheat the oven to 350°F/gas mark 4.

Pour the beans into a medium-sized high-sided oven dish.

Prepare the cornbread mix (see page 152) and pour evenly over the surface of the beans, leaving no gaps.

Bake in the hot oven for 20–25 minutes, until the cornbread is firm to touch and golden, or until a skewer inserted into the middle of the bread (not the beans!) comes out clean.

Mix together the ingredients for the chopped salad (see previous page).

Remove from the oven and serve with the chopped salad, sour cream and chili sauce if you like.

4 Romano peppers (the long
sweet ones), or 2 red or yellow
bell peppers, cut in half
lengthways and seeds removed

olive oil, to cook (about ½
teaspoon per half pepper)

TO ASSEMBLE
2½oz/¾ cup grated cheese,
Cheddar for example

5fl oz/⅔ cup sour cream

smoked paprika, to dust

Roasted in Peppers

Preheat the oven to 350°F/gas mark 4.

Lay the pepper halves cut side up in a baking tin or
dish, drizzle with olive oil and add a pinch of salt to
each cavity. Roast uncovered in the hot oven for 10
minutes, to soften.

Remove the peppers from the oven and fill each one to
not quite bursting with some of the beans. Top with a
good tablespoon of grated cheese, a teaspoon of sour
cream and a dusting of smoked paprika.

Position the peppers snugly back in the baking tin or
dish, propping them up alongside each other so the
beans don't spill out too much.

Bake in the oven for 15–20 minutes, until the beans are
bubbling and the pepper is soft, with the cheese and
cream dribbling and molten on top.

Mix together the ingredients for the chopped salad
(see page 55).

Remove the dish of peppers from the oven and serve at
the table with additional sour cream, chili sauce and
the chopped salad.

Butter Bean Paella

Studded with butter beans, this paella makes good use of the pantry: rice, canned beans and tomatoes, among others. A paella pan is ideal for this, but any wide, shallow pan will work.

Heat the oil in a wide, shallow pan over a moderate heat, then add the chicken/duck and pork ribs and brown all over for about 10 minutes. When it's nicely colored, reserve the browned meat on a plate.

Add the onion to the pan and cook to soften for at least 5 minutes, then add the garlic, paprika, tomatoes and the saffron with its soaking water.

Let the mixture cook for about 5 minutes, then return the fried meat to the pan, mixing well with a wooden spoon.

Add the stock or water and bring to a fierce boil, adding salt to taste (it should taste a bit saltier than you'd usually like, taking into account that the rice will absorb lots of flavor—about 1–1½ teaspoons is good).

Add the rice, shaking the pan so that the mixture evens out. Reduce the heat to moderate and from now on try not to stir the paella—this will help with producing the bottom crust (the socarrat) that makes for a good paella.

When the liquid has reduced by half (about 10 minutes), scatter the peas and butter beans over the surface of the paella.

Let the paella cook for about 20 minutes more, or until the rice is just cooked and the liquid has been fully absorbed.

Remove from the heat and rest the paella for at least 10 minutes.

Serve straight from the pan, scraping up the bottom bits, with some lemon wedges if you like.

3 tablespoons olive oil

2 chicken legs, chopped into small pieces through the bone (about 12 pieces in total)—or use duck if you'd rather

2 good-sized pork ribs, chopped into small pieces across the bone (ask your butcher to do this for you)

1 onion, finely diced

3 cloves of garlic, finely sliced

a generous pinch of sweet paprika

3 whole canned tomatoes, drained of juice and roughly chopped (approx. ½ a can)

a few strands of saffron, soaked in a little warm water for about 10 minutes

27fl oz/3½ cups chicken stock or water—hot but doesn't need to be boiling

14oz paella rice

4½oz/1 cup peas, fresh cooked or frozen

1 x 14oz can of butter beans, rinsed and drained

lemon wedges, to serve

White Beans with Toulouse Sausage, Broccoli and Garlic

White beans and broccoli are a wonderful combination—with the sausage and rosemary and so easy to make, this dish is a winner.

salt and freshly ground black pepper

1 large head of broccoli (about 1lb 2oz), broken up into smaller florets

2–3 tablespoons olive oil

4 Toulouse sausages (about 14oz), meat squeezed out roughly into chunks

1 large onion, finely diced

3 cloves of garlic, finely sliced

a good pinch of red pepper flakes, to taste

1 teaspoon fennel seeds, slightly crushed

1 good-sized sprig of fresh rosemary, leaves finely chopped

1 x 14oz can of cannellini or butter beans, rinsed and drained

a few shavings of Parmesan or Pecorino cheese per portion

1¾oz/just over ⅔ cup breadcrumbs, freshly toasted in a pan or in the oven

Bring a large pot of salted water to the boil. Cook the broccoli until tender, about 6 minutes, and drain well.

In a large pan, heat 1 tablespoon of olive oil over a medium-high heat. Add the sausage meat and cook, stirring often, for about 7 minutes, until the sausage is cooked through and beginning to brown in places. Remove the sausage from the pan with a slotted spoon, leaving behind the fat and any cooking juices. Set to one side.

Add another tablespoon of olive oil and the onion to the same frying pan and cook over a moderate heat for 8–10 minutes, until soft and translucent. Add the garlic, red pepper flakes, fennel seeds, rosemary and drained beans and stir over the heat so that the flavors meld and the mix begins to smell fragrant, about 2–3 minutes.

Add the cooked broccoli, mixing well. Taste for seasoning, adjusting with salt and pepper if necessary.

Divide the mix between bowls, topping each with some shavings of Parmesan or Pecorino, a drizzle of olive oil and the toasted breadcrumbs.

Black Turtle Bean and Beetroot Burgers

Serve these beet burgers with your choice of sour cream, mayonnaise, aïoli (see page 266), pickles (sliced gherkins are fabulous here), lettuce leaves, goat's cheese or feta. On rye bread or in a roll, find a combination that works for you.

1 onion, finely diced

1 tablespoon olive oil

2 cloves of garlic, finely sliced

2 medium beet (about 10½oz), peeled and grated

1 x 14oz can of black turtle beans, rinsed and drained, then roughly mashed with a fork

1 tablespoon Dijon mustard

½ teaspoon sweet paprika—smoked or unsmoked

1 teaspoon cumin seeds, toasted and ground

1 teaspoon coriander seeds, toasted and ground

a small bunch of fresh dill, leaves roughly chopped

3oz/just under 1 cup rolled oats—or use breadcrumbs, if you like

salt and freshly ground black pepper (about 1 teaspoon salt and ½ teaspoon pepper)

neutral cooking oil (sunflower or vegetable), for frying the burgers

Cook the onion in a small saucepan with the olive oil until soft and translucent, about 8–10 minutes, then add the garlic and cook for 2 minutes more, until fragrant. Remove from the heat and set to one side.

Combine the grated beet, beans, mustard, spices, dill, oats/breadcrumbs and seasoning in a bowl. Use your hands to work the mix together until cohesive and easily shaped.

Shape the mix into burgers about ¾ inch thick and place them on a tray or plate. Put them into the refrigerator to firm up for an hour or so.

Heat a large non-stick frying pan with enough oil to cover the surface of the pan and about ½ inch deep, and fry the burgers over a moderate heat for 2–3 minutes on each side, until crisp and the interior is hot.

Remove from the heat and serve immediately.

SLOW PULSES

Egyptian Ful Medames

1lb 2oz/4 cups whole dried fava beans, soaked in plenty of cold water overnight or throughout the day (or use canned fava)

salt and freshly ground black pepper

1 large red or white onion, finely diced

6 tablespoons vegetable oil

2–4 cloves of garlic, finely chopped, to taste

½–2 teaspoons red pepper flakes, to taste

3–4 teaspoons cumin seeds, toasted and ground, to taste

juice of 1 or 2 lemons

a large bunch of fresh parsley, roughly chopped, including any small stalks

TO SERVE
pita breads, toasted

hard-boiled eggs (see page 188)

chopped salad (see page 55)

chilli sauce (see page 169)

Serve this like they do for breakfast in Cairo, scooped into warm pita breads with halved hard-boiled eggs, tomatoes and cucumber. Make ful medames turbo-charged using plenty of chili and cumin, lots of lemon and garlic, and be generous with the chopped parsley. I've used vegetable oil here rather than olive oil because, for me, the flavor must be all about the fava, cumin, garlic, chili and lemon.

Put the soaked and drained beans into a large saucepan and cover with plenty of cold water. Bring to the boil, then reduce the heat to a simmer and cook for 45 minutes to 1 hour, or until the beans are tender. Add 1 tablespoon of salt to the bean cooking water in the last 5–10 minutes of cooking time. Take the beans off the heat and leave to cool in the liquid.

Meanwhile, in a saucepan over a moderate heat, fry the onion in 2 tablespoons of oil until soft and translucent, about 8–10 minutes. Add the garlic, red pepper flakes and cumin and cook for a further 2 minutes.

Add the cooked beans to the onion, using some of the bean cooking liquid to loosen the mix if desired. You want it thick, but still a little soupy and fluid.

Continue to warm the beans through in the onion over a low heat for about 10 minutes.

Remove about a third of the beans and blend, returning the blended mix back to the whole bean mix. Stir to combine. (This stage is optional—you can omit the blending of the beans, keeping them all whole if you prefer.)

Stir in the lemon juice, parsley and about 2–4 more tablespoons of oil, tasting the beans for seasoning, adjusting with salt, pepper, lemon and more spice as needed. Serve warm or at room temperature, with pita breads, hard-boiled eggs, chopped salad and chili sauce. Think of the ful medames as a robustly textured and vigorously flavored mezze or dip.

7oz/about 1⅓ cups whole dried
fava beans, soaked in plenty
of cold water overnight or
throughout the day (or use
tinned fava)

1 clove of garlic, finely chopped

1 small onion, finely diced

a large bunch of fresh cilantro,
long stalks removed and finely
chopped, leaves roughly chopped

a large bunch of fresh parsley,
long stalks removed and finely
chopped, leaves roughly chopped

1 teaspoon coriander seeds,
toasted and ground

1 teaspoon cumin seeds, toasted
and ground

½ teaspoon salt

½ teaspoon black pepper or red
pepper flakes, or to taste

sunflower oil, for frying the falafel

tahini sauce (see opposite),
to serve

Falafel

**Serve these falafel stuffed into toasted pita breads
with tahini sauce (see opposite); add chopped
tomato and cucumber, seasoned yogurt and also
some chili sauce (see page 169).**

Rinse the soaked fava beans, then drain well and put
into a food processor. Add the garlic, onion, herbs,
spices, salt and chili flakes/pepper and blend with
about 3½fl oz/⅓ cup of water until you have a smooth
green paste.

Heat a little oil in a frying pan over a moderate heat and
fry a teaspoon of the mixture to check the seasoning.
Adjust with more salt and/or red pepper flakes/pepper
if necessary. Chill the mixture in the refrigerator for at
least 30 minutes.

Preheat the oven to about 300°F/gas mark 3.

Heat some oil in a medium-sized and high-sided
saucepan—about a 2-inch depth of oil is good—
until very hot. If you have a digital thermometer, the
temperature of the oil should be about 350°F. The
mixture is quite wet and the oil is very hot, so be careful
here. Using two dessert spoons, one to shape and one
to scrape the mixture off, drop a spoonful of the batter
into the hot oil—it should bubble and fry, quickly
turning crisp and golden brown. Flip the falafel over
to fry on the other side. Work in small batches, 3 or 4
at a time, removing the falafel with a slotted spoon
when crisp.

Reserve the cooked falafel on a plate or baking dish in
the warm oven and continue to fry the rest of the mix.

When the falafel mix is all used up, serve the falafel with
the tahini sauce.

Tahini Sauce

½ a clove of garlic, crushed to a smooth paste with a pinch of salt

1¾oz/¼ cup tahini

1 tablespoon extra virgin olive oil

juice of ½ a lemon

salt and freshly ground black pepper

Combine the garlic, tahini and oil in a small bowl.

Add the lemon juice, then whisk in 3½fl oz/⅓ cup of water a spoonful at a time, stirring briskly between additions to make a smooth sauce. The consistency should be like heavy cream.

Season to taste with salt and pepper.

9oz/1½–2 cups dried black turtle beans, soaked in plenty of cold water overnight

3 bay leaves

4 tablespoons olive oil

1 onion, finely diced

1 green bell pepper, deseeded and finely diced

5½oz smoked bacon, cut into thin strips

3 cloves of garlic, finely sliced

1 teaspoon ground cumin

½–1 teaspoon dried oregano

salt and freshly ground black pepper

1 tablespoon red wine vinegar or lime juice, to taste

TO GARNISH, BARE MINIMUM

sour cream

red onion, finely sliced

red or green bell peppers, deseeded and finely chopped

OTHER OPTIONAL GARNISHES
banana, chopped

red pepper flakes or chopped fresh chili

cilantro leaves, roughly chopped

avocado, chopped

fresh tomato, diced

sweetcorn

Black Turtle Bean and Bacon Soup with Chop Chop and Sour Cream

Ham bones, if you, your butcher or your delicatessen have any, are a welcome addition here when you cook the beans. An inky-rich black turtle bean soup, smoky with bacon and sweet with bell peppers, it's best of all when you serve this soup with as many garnishes as you can muster—think bright colors and contrasting textures.

Drain the soaked beans, rinse under cold water, then drain again and put into a large deep pan with enough fresh cold water to cover the beans by at least 2 inches. Add the bay leaves and bring to the boil over a high heat. Skim off any froth that appears, then reduce the heat to low and simmer, covered slightly, for 1½–2 hours, or until the beans are tender. If the beans get too dry, top up with more water.

While the beans are cooking, heat the olive oil in a saucepan and add the diced onion, green bell pepper and bacon. Cook over a moderate heat for 8–10 minutes, until the onion and pepper are soft. Add the garlic, cumin and oregano, with 1 teaspoon of salt and a generous quantity of black pepper. Cook for a further 3–4 minutes, so that the flavors meld and the mix starts to become soft and sweet-smelling. Put to one side.

When the beans are cooked, drain, reserving the cooking liquid. Add the beans to the onion and bacon mix, stirring to combine, adding cupfuls of the bean cooking liquid to the bean mix until you have the desired consistency.

At this point you can partially blend the soup—remove about a quarter or a third and blend, returning the blended mix to the unblended beans and stirring—or you can leave it as it is.

Taste the soup, adjusting with salt and pepper where necessary and adding 1 tablespoon or so of red wine vinegar or lime juice to season.

Serve immediately, with your choice of garnish.

7oz/about 1⅓ cups dried borlotti beans, soaked in plenty of cold water overnight or throughout the day

½ bulb of garlic, unpeeled

a big bunch of fresh sage, about 15 leaves

½–1 teaspoon red pepper flakes (optional)

3 whole tomatoes (use canned, drained of juice)

4–6 tablespoons olive oil

salt and freshly ground black pepper

Dried Beans Cooked under Oil and Water with Sage

This is a very simple method, with the tomato, garlic and sage all permeating the beans as they cook. Borlotti beans are best, but any dried beans will work. Just keep an eye on the water levels as you bake the beans. Use a casserole dish if you like, but a wide roasting pan covered with foil works just as well. Gorgeous alongside roasted meats or thrown into salads.

Preheat the oven to 400°F/gas mark 6.

Put the drained beans, garlic, sage leaves, red pepper flakes and tomatoes into a casserole dish that will accommodate your beans comfortably—and fit in your oven!

Add enough cold water to cover the beans by at least 2 inches. Add the olive oil, enough to cover the surface with a good film of oil.

Add the lid or cover with foil and bake in the oven for 1–3 hours, until the beans are tender. You may want to check in on them from time to time and top up with a bit more water.

When the beans are soft, remove from the oven and season with salt and pepper to taste.

To serve, drain the cooked beans and dress with a little lemon juice and some extra olive oil with salt and pepper to taste.

Puglian Garbanzo Beans with Rosemary and Black Olives

Use soaked dried split fava beans here if you prefer them to garbanzo beans. Rich and comforting, this is a staple dish of southern Italy. Use best-quality olive oil to scent the mash. The garlic boils with the garbanzo beans, turning sweet and creamy, and the olives and chili give a salty heat to the greens and mashed pulses.

7oz/1 cup dried garbanzo beans, soaked in plenty of cold water overnight or throughout the day

5 cloves of garlic, unpeeled and left whole, plus 2 cloves, finely chopped

1 onion, finely diced

1 whole dried chili (not too hot)

salt and freshly ground black pepper

2½fl oz/⅓ cup olive oil, plus extra to serve

9oz chard, spinach or turnip tops (Italian bitter greens are best of all), washed and drained

a pinch of red pepper flakes, plus extra to serve

1 good-sized sprig of fresh rosemary, leaves finely chopped

1¾–2¾oz/about ½ cup pitted black olives, roughly chopped

Put the drained garbanzo beans into a large deep-sided pan with enough fresh cold water to cover them by at least 2 inches. Add the whole garlic cloves, the onion and the whole chili and bring to the boil over a high heat. Turn down the heat to a simmer, then cover the pan and cook for about 1–2 hours, or until the garbanzo beans are soft. If the pan gets too dry, top up with a little more cold water.

Once cooked, drain the garbanzo beans, reserving the cooking water. Discard the whole chili and pop the garlic flesh out of the skins, discarding the skin. The onion will have long disintegrated.

Put the garbanzo beans and squeezed-out garlic into a blender or food processor, or use a stick blender, and add 1 teaspoon of salt and lots of freshly ground black pepper, to taste. Blend, adding about three-quarters of the olive oil, until you reach the desired consistency. I like mine a little bit lumpy, but you can process until smooth if you like.

Cook the chard, spinach or other green vegetables in plenty of salted water for 2 minutes, or until just tender. Drain, then run under cold water and squeeze out any excess water.

Fry the chopped garlic, red pepper flakes and rosemary in the remaining olive oil for 1 minute. Add the blanched greens to the chili, garlic, rosemary and oil and season well with salt and pepper to taste.

To serve, put the garbanzo bean purée on a large plate and top with the fried greens. Drizzle with the oil from the pan and scatter with the chopped olives. More red pepper flakes might be nice too.

3 GRAINS

When I first started cooking professionally I remember reading about a salad made in part with pearl barley—the author referred appreciatively to the dish as more of a rubble than a salad. In that moment I knew I wanted to write about food as well as cook it for a living. A greedy reading habit ensued and I found myself reading everything 'food' I could get my hands on. Books, weekend newspaper supplements, journals and magazines; supply and demand, my pace of cooking was remarkable. The more I read, the more I cooked. Making the connection between reading great food writing and developing at the time as a chef—becoming more experienced and ambitious with different ingredients—was, and still is, empowering. Soon enough both my bookshelves and pantry began to swell. I have always been a fan of cookbooks in the kitchen, well thumbed and food-splattered. I like the ebb and flow of books as they make their way from bookshelf to workhorse, slap bang in the middle of the kitchen table. With cookbooks comes possibility, almost as if we can travel the world through the contents of our kitchen.

With rubble as a curious impetus to read more, cook more and write more, what I continue to like about the word and all it conjures for me in a culinary sense is to use ingredients as a tumbling assembly of flavor. In so far as grains are concerned, they are economical and versatile. Plumped by cooking, grains are a brilliant canvas for flavor. Incentive to use grains in different applications comes by way of whatever meat, fish, vegetables, cheese or herbs you may have to hand. Additional seasoning and the knack of bringing the dish together is helped along with the everyday staples of olive oil, butter, tahini, spices, seeds, nuts and yogurt, to name a few.

I love to use grains in my cooking as pearly ballast to chomp and savor. Nubby and nutritious, scattergun swollen cooked grains work well in chunky seasonal salads. The spelt, pumpkin and bacon one (see page 100) or wheat grains with fava beans, peas and tahini (see page 95) are both good examples. Served just warm or at room temperature, dishes like these make me feel like I am cheating in the kitchen. Not really cooking, just harnessing ingredients in a bowl.

Grains also triumph when cooked as one, and risotto is the finest example of all. Nurtured from the off, risotto rice grains are toasted with a little butter or olive oil, some softened onion and sometimes garlic, hit with wine, then good stock, and stirred, stirred, stirred. A superb risotto can be made of so few ingredients, improved only by the addition of some Parmesan and more glorious butter beaten through at the very end. In its most simple form, risotto is the ultimate in pantry staples, and risotto Milanese is a belter. Flashed through with saffron, the grains of rice are suspended in their own creamy cooking liquid, like magma, golden on a plate. Risotto has an intimidating reputation. It needn't have, but it is true that you will need to stand there stoveside stirring and coaxing the grains for the full 18 or so minutes it takes for the rice to cook to the point of perfection. Wine helps, as does a good wooden spoon, well versed in stirring.

If risotto is considered high-maintenance grain cookery, pilafs are the opposite. Fragrant with spice, sometimes jewelled with nuts and dried fruit among others, the rice is first toasted in the hot fat to lock the grain into shape before the interior begins to steam in the liquid. With lid tight shut, it is left well alone on the hob or in the oven—nothing can escape. Rice cooked, lid lifted, the pot then gives an intoxicating, gloriously perfumed, steamy belch. Middle Eastern inspired rice cookery is a firm favorite and, hands down, for me and the way I like to cook at home, a winning way with rice. Best of all is the sought-after crunchy crispy bottom layer of rice from the pot known as the tah-dig ('bottom of the pot' in the Persian/Farsi language). Families have long fought over who gets to eat this bronzed crust, and will no doubt continue to do so for as long as pots and rice and liquid meet over heat.

Porridge as a term is ambiguous. At its most prosaic, porridge can mean any cooked mush of cereal, pulses or grains. It can also include meat, fish and vegetables. In the context of grains cooked in liquid, cornmeal (polenta) or oats (porridge) and also lentils as a pulse (dhal) all fall into this category and make fantastic use of grains and pulses in wet, soupy preparations. Congee—rice cooked in liquid with the addition of flavour, where the rice is cooked so much it begins to disintegrate—is also a porridge of sorts. More typically though, I suppose, porridge is best known to refer to oatmeal. It is a sure-fire family breakfast and one I'm thankful for come the wintry months. In my cooking, I am also keen to make use of oats in more ways than just porridge. To bind or coat ingredients before baking or frying, or even blitzed dry in a blender, oats can make a brilliant alternative to flours and ground nuts, for example.

Housed in jars, packets and practical though ugly plastic containers, I like the chalky pleasure to be had when scooping out grains for use. I like too that there is something timeless and gratifying in the feeling of grains as they rain through your hands into a bowl to soak or a pan to boil. Barley was a one-time currency represented by the old Israeli shekel coinage. So prized as a foodstuff, each coin bore reference to its commercial weight in grain. In the Khmer language, the verb 'to eat' literally means 'to eat rice' and 'hungry' translates as 'hungry for rice'. Rice is a universal ingredient and is said to supply over half of all humankind's calorie intake.

Grains have long signified an important part of our diet and represent a vital food source. I couldn't imagine my pantry without them. Interchangeable in some recipes, I would encourage you to buy and cook with different grains and use these recipes as building blocks. Grain cookery in whichever direction you head, whatever flavors you use, is always satisfying.

PANTRY BASICS

Basmati rice

risotto (Arborio, Carnaroli,
Vialone Nano) rice

brown rice

short-grain (pudding) rice

rolled (porridge) oats

pinhead oatmeal

farro

freekeh

bulgur, coarse and fine

spelt

barley, pearl and pot

Rice comes in three different sizes: long, medium and short grain. Long-grain rice is slim and produces tender grains that remain firm but fluffy when cooked. Best known and highly prized is Basmati rice. Medium-grain rice is wider and shorter and is used in the moist, chewy rice dishes of risotto and paella. Short-grain rice is a tubby plump grain that cooks soft and is suited to puddings and sushi.

A rice grain has seven layers. Brown rice is the whole grain with only its outermost layer, the hull, removed. White rice is made by milling, polishing and processing brown rice to make it white. Brown rice takes longer to cook than white, but the health benefits are total. With staggering nutritional value, brown rice is listed as one of the world's healthiest foods. I enjoy the nutty toothsome characteristics of brown rice but still couldn't be without white in my pantry. Indeed, the smell of white rice as it cooks is a favorite kitchen aroma. The steamy vapor as it bubbles and puffs beneath pan and lid tells me all is well.

Having both varieties on your shelf is a given. When cooking plain rice of both hues, I will often cook double the amount and reserve any leftovers in the refrigerator to use up in the next 2 or 3 days. Cooked rice is a quick and invaluable ingredient to have to hand for stir-fries and dressed in salads. Simple tips for cooking plain rice: toasting the grains in a hot pan or in the oven until fragrant before adding any liquid will boost their flavor, using stock to cook the grains rather than just water will intensify a dish, and, finally, try adding whole spices along with the liquid as the grains cook, gently perfuming the rice.

Breakfast, lunch and supper, rice does it all.

Brown Porridge with Coconut Milk, Brown Sugar and Cinnamon

This stuff is magic and a brilliant way to use up leftover cooked brown rice. Alternatively you may want to cook brown rice especially for this recipe: it is worth the effort.

10½oz/2¼ cups brown rice, boiled in plenty of water until soft (about 40–50 minutes)

1 x 14fl oz can of coconut milk

4 tablespoons desiccated coconut

salt

¼ teaspoon ground ginger

½ teaspoon freshly grated nutmeg

1 teaspoon ground cinnamon

brown sugar (or maple syrup or honey), to taste

Put the rice into a large pot and mix with the coconut milk, desiccated coconut and 7fl oz/just under 1 cup of water.

Bring to the boil, then let it simmer, uncovered, for 20 minutes. Stir occasionally (about every 5 minutes).

Add a pinch of salt and the spices, give it a good stir, and cook for 5 more minutes, or until the desired consistency is reached, adding sweetening to taste.

Serve warm.

5 teaspoons vegetable oil

9oz/2¼ cups beansprouts

salt

5½oz/3 cups shredded green or
white cabbage

2 large carrots, peeled and very
thinly sliced lengthways

10½oz/4½ cups mushrooms,
stemmed and thinly sliced

3 cloves of garlic, finely chopped

14oz beef or pork mince

2 inches fresh ginger, minced

1 clove of garlic, minced

1lb 7oz/about 3 cups short-grain
brown rice, cooked as per packet
instructions, warm

TO SERVE

½ a bunch of green onions, thinly
sliced, for garnish

3 tablespoons sesame oil

1 tablespoon sesame seeds

4 fried eggs (optional)

kimchi

gochujang (Korean red pepper
paste)—or use chili oil (see page
169) or sriracha

cucumber batons

Brown Rice Bibimbap

A traditional Korean rice dish, bibimbap means
'mixed rice' and typically includes a mixture of sautéed
vegetables, often a fried egg, and/or some fried meat.
Gochujang is a spicy fermented chili and red pepper
paste that will keep in the refrigerator for up to a year,
but if you can't get hold of any, use chili sauce (see
page 169). Very little beats the furious enjoyment of a
bibimbap table cluttered with different dishes, everyone
digging deep to embellish their own rice bowl.

Preheat a wok on a high heat and warm 1 tablespoon
of the oil. Add the beansprouts and cook for 1 minute,
until just wilted. Season lightly with salt, then transfer to
a bowl and wipe out the wok with some kitchen paper.

Repeat with the cabbage, cooking it for 2–3 minutes.
Season lightly with salt and reserve in a bowl or on
a plate. Use a little more oil as needed throughout
this process.

Repeat with the carrots and reserve.

Finally repeat with the mushrooms, adding the garlic
and cooking until the mushrooms have released all their
liquid, then continue to cook until the mushrooms are
dry. Transfer to a bowl or plate.

If you want to include the fried meat, fry the mince in a
little oil in the hot wok (like the vegetables), along with
the minced fresh ginger and garlic. Cook until any liquid
evaporates. Reserve in a bowl.

Wipe out the wok and reheat with the remaining oil
until hot, then add the cooked warm rice and gently
press it down with a spatula. Cook over a moderate
heat, without stirring, until the rice is crisp beneath—
this should take about 3–4 minutes. Give it a quick stir
through and leave to fry for 1 or 2 minutes more before
removing from the heat.

Turn the rice out on to a large plate and serve at the
table with as many additional dishes as you can muster.
More the merrier!

2 tablespoons vegetable oil

1 block of firm tofu, cut into ¾-inch chunks

2 tablespoons soy sauce

4 tablespoons white miso paste

2 tablespoons sesame oil

1 tablespoon rice vinegar

1 tablespoon brown sugar

1¼ inches fresh ginger, unpeeled and finely grated

2 cloves of garlic, grated or crushed

14oz/3 cups edamame, shelled, cooked for 1 minute in boiling water, then drained

3 carrots, thinly sliced

1lb 7oz/about 3 cups cooked brown long-grain rice

2 green onions, finely chopped

3 tablespoons toasted sesame seeds

Brown Rice, Edamame and Miso

Miso is another refrigerator stalwart with a good shelf life. A Japanese ingredient made from fermented soybeans, it is rich in vitamins, protein and minerals. Miso paste is superior in taste and texture to dried miso, which exists in packet form for a speedy fix. Diluted with boiling water to make soup, it is widely recognized as a fast-food staple in Japan. Here miso paste is mixed with the rice and beans, with savory and satisfying results. Tofu is a welcome addition to the mix, but not essential.

Heat a non-stick pan over a medium-high heat. Add half the vegetable oil and then the tofu chunks. Fry until lightly browned on all sides, turning occasionally. Stir in 1 tablespoon of soy sauce to deglaze the pan and stir well. Set the tofu aside to cool on a plate.

In a small bowl, whisk together the miso, the remaining soy sauce, the sesame oil, rice vinegar, 2 tablespoons of water and the brown sugar until smooth.

Heat the remaining vegetable oil in the pan over a medium-high heat. Add the ginger and garlic and fry for 1 minute, then add half the miso mixture and whisk until heated through. Add the edamame and carrots and cook together for 1 minute. Remove from the heat and transfer to the tofu plate.

Return the pan to the heat and add the rice, stirring to heat through. When the rice is hot, remove from the heat and add the edamame and carrots, the tofu and finally the green onions and sesame seeds.

Serve the rice mix in a large bowl, with the rest of the miso mixture poured over the top.

Kheema Biryani

Kheema is a South Asian dish using minced meat. Fried and mixed with yogurt before being baked in a Basmati bed and blanket, this biryani method is as fascinating as it is failsafe. With the meat marinating in the yogurt, you get soft, tender mince scented with mesmerizing rose water, almond and spices.

Cook the rice in a medium saucepan without a lid with 1 teaspoon of salt, 9fl oz/1 cup of water and the whole spices until it is just half done and the liquid has all evaporated. Drain in a large colander, then spread the rice evenly on a large dish to dry out a little.

Meanwhile mix the saffron with the warm milk and set aside, adding a few drops of rose water if using.

Heat the butter or oil in a deep pan over a moderate heat, then add the sliced onion and bay leaves and fry until the onion is soft and translucent, about 8–10 minutes.

Mix in the minced lamb, ginger, garlic, red pepper flakes, and cumin and fry for a further 10 minutes over a slightly lower, medium heat. Take off the heat and leave to cool for 10 minutes, then add the yogurt and stir well.

Preheat the oven to 350°F/gas mark 4.

Spread half the pre-cooked rice in a casserole or heavy-bottomed pan for which you have a lid. Spread the cooked lamb yogurt mix over the rice and pour over the saffron milk. Grate the nutmeg to your taste, all over the dish. Cover with the remaining rice and top with the raisins and almonds.

Put the lid on the pan and cook in the hot oven for another 30–35 minutes, until the liquid has all evaporated and the rice is tender.

Remove from the oven and set aside to rest for 5 minutes. Serve with seasoned yogurt (plain yogurt mixed with some salt and a little garlic) and some hot pickles or chutney.

9oz/about 1¼ cups Basmati rice

salt

1 cinnamon stick

5 cloves

4 green cardamom pods

10 black peppercorns

a few strands of saffron

3½fl oz/⅓ cup milk, warm

rose water—depending on strength, a few drops and up to 1 teaspoon (optional)

5 tablespoons melted butter or vegetable oil (use ghee if you like)

1 large onion, sliced

2 bay leaves

12oz minced lamb

¾ inch fresh ginger, grated

2 cloves of garlic, finely chopped

1 teaspoon red pepper flakes or powder

1 teaspoon ground cumin

2oz/¼ cup yogurt, plus extra to serve

¼–½ nutmeg, to grate

3 tablespoons each of raisins and chopped almonds

10½oz/1½ cups Basmati rice

3 tablespoons butter

1 onion, thinly sliced

3 teaspoons in total of ground spices—choose from coriander, cumin, pepper, turmeric, ginger, allspice, nutmeg, cardamom (use less of a measure if choosing from the last 3 listed)

1 cinnamon stick

2¾oz/½ cup dried sour cherries (or dried cranberries)

salt

3½oz/¾ cup shelled pistachios (or almond flakes)

8fl oz/1 cup chicken stock, boiling, plus 8fl oz/1 cup water, boiling (16fl oz/2 cups) in all, or use all water if you like)

TO SERVE

7oz/1 cup plain yogurt

1 small clove of garlic, crushed

2 teaspoons sumac (optional)

a medium bunch of herbs, leaves roughly chopped—parsley, dill or mint, or a combination

1 teaspoon red pepper flakes, or to taste

lemon wedges

Sour Cherry and Pistachio Pilaf

Heaven is a pilaf that makes everyone want to eat everything. This is my current favorite version: seductive, noble, and very, very beautiful. Ideally, toast the whole spices before you grind them.

Wash the Basmati rice thoroughly and drain well.

Heat the butter in a pan over a medium heat, then add the onion and sauté for 8–10 minutes, until it turns completely soft. Add the spices, cherries and a generous pinch of salt and cook for 1 minute more.

Add the rice and pistachios and give a good stir over the heat for a minute or 2 to toast the rice, then add the liquid and check the seasoning.

Put a lid on the pan and cook the rice on high for 3 minutes, then turn the heat down to low and continue to cook for 15 more minutes, until all the liquid has evaporated and the rice is tender.

Take off the heat. Place a clean dish towel between pan and lid and let the pan sit and rest for 5 minutes. The dish towel will help draw excess moisture from the pan and helps to keep the rice extra fluffy.

While the rice is cooking, season the yogurt with a bit of salt, the garlic and the sumac, if using.

When the rice is ready to serve, with a fork stir through the majority of the herbs, fluffing the rice as you go.

Serve the pilaf at the table, with the yogurt, red pepper flakes, remaining herbs and lemons to add per bowlful.

Risotto Milanese

You'll need some good stock, but everything else is worthy of a pantry staple.

2¼oz/just over ¼ cup butter

1 small white onion, finely diced

14oz/2 cups risotto rice (Arborio, Carnaroli, Vialone Nano)

2 generous pinches of saffron strands

salt and freshly ground black pepper

6fl oz/¾ cup dry white wine, about 1 glass

1¾ pints/4½ cups chicken stock, hot (use 50:50 with water, or use 100% veg stock or water if you prefer)

3oz/1 cup freshly grated Parmesan cheese

In a heavy-bottomed saucepan, melt half the butter over a moderate heat. Add the onion and cook until soft and translucent, 8–10 minutes.

Add the rice, saffron and ½ teaspoon of salt, turning the heat up slightly. Move the rice about the pan, coating the grains and saffron strands in the hot fat. Do this for about 2 minutes.

Add the wine and your pan will give a gasp, absorbing all the wine. Stir until all the wine has evaporated.

Reduce the heat back to moderate and add the first ladleful of hot stock to the pan. Stir continuously until all the liquid has evaporated.

Repeat with another ladleful of stock, stirring until evaporated.

Do this until most or all of the stock is used up. Check the rice continually from about 12 minutes into the cooking time. You want the grains to be tender but with a modicum of bite left in the very center.

When the rice is ready, add the remaining butter and half the Parmesan. Beat like you mean it! The risotto should be glossy and creamy. Take off the heat, put the lid on and rest the pan for 5 minutes.

Serve at the table with the remaining Parmesan to add per person—perfect consistency for risotto is when you add a portion to the plate and the risotto just glides across the surface. It shouldn't clump or be swimming in liquid. Like magma, semi-fluid.

OATS

A principal cereal crop for Scotland and Wales, oats thrive in cool temperate regions high in moisture, where other crops might fail. Whole and unbroken, grain groats (the inner portion of the oat kernel) are gluten-free, with higher levels of fat than many other grains. Higher fat levels do mean that oats have a shorter shelf life than other grains, so buy little and often.

Groats are milled to a variety of grades: pinhead, rough, medium rough, medium fine and superfine. Most useful to have on your shelves? My oat use is twofold. For cooking and baking, the commonly available rolled or jumbo oats are my choice. Soft and pliable, they prove an endlessly useful standby in quick-cook porridge, granolas, flapjacks, biscuits, smoothies, muffins or bircher muesli, or blitzed into a wheat flour alternative. For porridge superior in both texture and flavor, it's got to be pinhead—steel cut, or Irish. These are groats that are cut in half and still have their fibrous bran attached. Soaking these oats overnight before cooking will improve the finished texture, but even without soaking these oats can cook to a porridge in 30 or so minutes. Follow the packet instructions and experiment with what you serve with your morning bowl of porridge: chopped nuts, toasted seeds, dried and fresh fruits, maple syrup or honey, spices and fruit compotes. Or go savory and make the baked oatmeal on page 90 for brunch.

3½oz/½ cup rolled, jumbo or steel cut/pinhead porridge oats (your usual porridge preference)

salt

1 bunch asparagus, woody ends removed

1½oz/just under ¼ cup butter

4 eggs

3oz/about ½ cup freshly grated Parmesan cheese

1 teaspoon pimentón—hot or sweet, as you like

Baked Oatmeal with Eggs, Asparagus and Pimentón

Chewy and creamy, oats make a terrific substitute for potatoes or bread in this dish. Use spinach instead of asparagus if you like. Also, bacon fried in the hot butter before adding the layer of porridge is sensational.

Make the porridge as per the packet instructions, adding ½ teaspoon of salt as it cooks. If you're using steel cut/pinhead oats you'll need more time to make this recipe.

Preheat the oven to 400°F/gas mark 6.

In a pan of boiling water, cook the asparagus for 2–3 minutes, until just cooked.

Put the butter into a non-stick ovenproof frying pan/skillet and melt over a moderate heat.

With the pan hot and the butter foaming, add the cooked porridge to the frying pan/skillet, spreading it out roughly.

Arrange the cooked asparagus spears over the surface of the porridge, pushing them in slightly.

Make 4 pockets in the surface of the porridge and asparagus and crack an egg into each.

Sprinkle with the cheese and pimentón.

Put the frying pan into the oven and cook until the whites are set and yolks still runny. This will only take a few minutes so keep an eye on them.

Remove from the oven and serve straight from the pan. I like to eat this with chili sauce (see page 169) or some gojuchang (Korean red pepper paste).

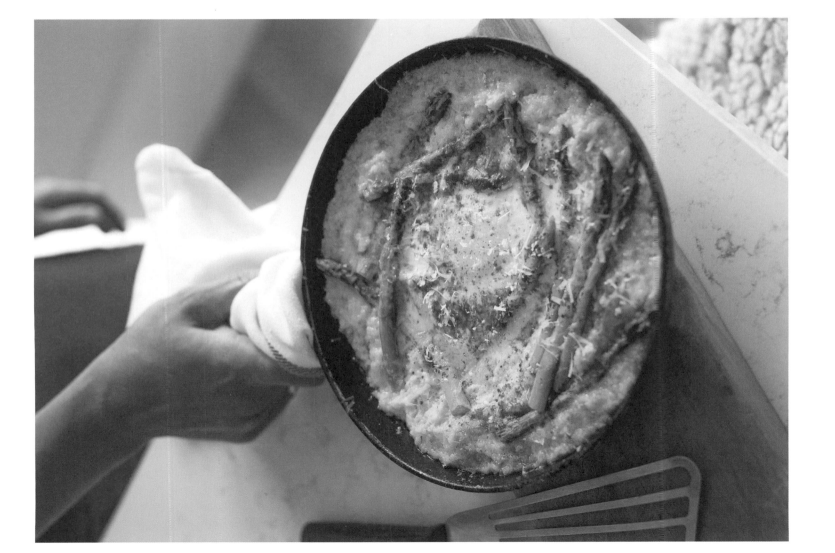

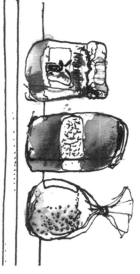

Oat, Black Pudding, Carrot and Parsley Patties

I can't bring myself to call these 'mini burgers'. Neither do I think they can go by the name of fritters. Patties is more apt: a pleasing, old-fashioned sort of word. Black pudding contains oats and is a wonderful ingredient to have in your refrigerator. Crumbled and bound with more oats and eggs here, these fried tubby disks are great. Serve hot from the pan, stuffed into a baguette with a leaf or two of soft, buttery lettuce, maybe even some mayonnaise or aïoli (see page 266).

1 large onion, finely diced

vegetable oil, for frying

1lb black pudding, skin removed and crumbled

1lb carrots, peeled and grated

a small bunch of fresh flat-leaf parsley, leaves finely chopped

6 tablespoons oats (about ½ cup), plus extra to coat

2 eggs, beaten

salt and freshly ground black pepper to taste—about ½ teaspoon salt and ½ teaspoon pepper is good

MAKES AROUND 10–12

Fry the onion until soft and translucent in a spot of oil, about 8–10 minutes. Set aside to cool.

Put the black pudding and grated carrots into a bowl and add the cooked onion, parsley, oats, eggs and salt and pepper using your hands to fully combine the mix together.

Put the mix into the refrigerator for 30 minutes to firm up.

To test the mix for seasoning, fry a small portion in a frying pan with a spot of oil, and taste. Add more salt and pepper if necessary.

Sprinkle a large plate with more oats and shape the mix into little rounds, coating each in oats.

Oil the surface of a large frying pan over a moderate heat, and fry the patties for 2–3 minutes each side, until crisp and hot throughout. Don't overcrowd the pan—work in batches, reserving the cooked patties on a warm and waiting plate lined with some kitchen paper.

Serve immediately, as above (see introduction).

Oat and Golden Syrup Tart

Oats and golden syrup are meant for each other. On porridge, in flapjacks and here in this tart with apples.

3¼oz/about 1 cup rolled oats

4¼oz/just under 1 cup walnuts

2¾oz/about ¼ cup golden syrup

5oz/½ cup butter, diced

a pinch of salt

4 small apples, cored and sliced into rounds ½ inch thick

½ teaspoon ground cinnamon

¼ teaspoon freshly grated nutmeg

MAKES 1 X 9-INCH TART

Grind the oats in a food processor or blender until a fine flour forms. Pour the oat flour into a bowl and add the walnuts to the processor. Process until finely ground (be sure to stop before it becomes walnut butter!). Add the walnut mix to the bowl.

Put two-thirds of the golden syrup and 3¾oz/just over ¼ cup of the butter into a small pan over a moderate heat and warm through to melt the butter.

Add the warm golden syrup and butter to the ground oats and walnuts with the salt. Mix until the butter is fully incorporated, then gather the crust into a ball, wrap in plastic wrap and refrigerate for 30 minutes to firm up.

Preheat the oven to 350°F/gas mark 4.

Press the crust into the bottom and up the sides of a 9-inch tart tin with a removable base. Bake for 10 minutes, until firm.

Arrange the apples in overlapping concentric circles on the bottom of the baked crust. Add the cinnamon and nutmeg and drizzle the remaining golden syrup all over the spiced apples. Dot the top of the apples evenly with the remaining diced butter.

Bake the tart for 20 minutes. Test an apple for tenderness with a skewer or sharp knife—if it isn't easily pierced, continue baking for another 5–10 minutes. You want the apples to be tender. If the crust begins to color too much as the apples cook, cover the edges with some foil.

Remove from the oven and let the tart stand for 10 minutes before slicing. Serve with chilled cream, ice cream, crème fraîche or custard.

WHOLE WHEAT GRAIN:
FARRO, FREEKEH OR BULGUR

Like the other grains, wheat can be enjoyed as a wholegrain and not just as a flour in baking. Whole wheat kernels can take up to an hour to cook, less if you soak them for an hour in warm water beforehand. To cook farro, wheat berries or whole grain wheat, follow the packet instructions, adding salt at the end of the cooking time so as to not toughen the grains as they cook. Boil until tender but still with a chewy bite. With the bran, germ and endosperm intact, these wheat grains are high in fiber and contain a staggeringly healthy balance of nutrients. Use as you would any other wholegrain, in soups, stews and dressed in salads.

Freekeh is a little different in form, as is bulgur wheat. Freekeh is wheat grain harvested while the grains are still green, set alight, smoked within the husk, then roasted and thrashed to disperse the flavour before being cracked into smaller pieces resembling broken wheat grains. Popular in the Middle East and North Africa, freekeh is prized for its rich, nutty, smoky flavour. Bulgur is dried cracked durum wheat and is a phenomenally popular ingredient throughout the Arabic-speaking world. It can be purchased in a coarse and fine grind, with the latter's cooking time considerably shorter. I find bulgur more interesting in flavor and texture than extruded durum wheat in the form of couscous. With a longer cooking time, bulgur can be interchangeable with couscous in many recipes; have both on your shelves.

While spelt is a member of the grain family, it is not the same species as wheat. Many people with a sensitivity to wheat find it a more tolerable grain to digest. Buy wholegrain spelt and use in lieu of wheat for many recipes, such as the fava bean and tahini number (opposite). Recipes, like ingredients, do not have to be absolute (finicky pâtisserie work withstanding); a little give and take, this and that, makes for more interesting cooking and certainly helps with the art of stocking a pantry. Switch grains around in this set of recipes if you like; if a particular grain is intrinsic to the dish, I'll let you know.

Wheat Grains with Fava Beans and Tahini

9oz/1½ cups whole wheat grain—farro, freekeh or coarse bulgur

3 tablespoons olive oil, plus extra for drizzling

salt and freshly ground black pepper

7oz/1 cup Greek yogurt

juice of 1 lemon

3 teaspoons cumin seeds, toasted and ground

6 tablespoons tahini

1 clove of garlic, crushed

14oz podded fava beans (or trimmed asparagus, peas, or a combination)

a generous bunch of fresh cilantro, stalks and leaves separated, stalks finely chopped, leaves roughly chopped

red pepper flakes

Cook the wheat as per the instructions on the packet. Bulgur will have the shortest cooking time, wholegrain wheat or farro the longest, with freekeh somewhere in the middle. Drain, and put the warm cooked grains into a mixing bowl. Add the olive oil and season with salt and pepper to taste.

For the dressing, blend together the yogurt, lemon juice, cumin, tahini, 2¼fl oz of water and the garlic and season with salt and pepper.

Meanwhile cook the fava beans in a pan of salted water for 2–6 minutes (depending on the size, drain and peel the skin off any which are larger than a thumbnail).

To serve, add approximately two-thirds of the fava beans and the cilantro stalks to the cooked grains, mixing well. Stir in the dressing, tasting for seasoning and adjusting if necessary.

Spread the salad out on a wide serving plate (shown overleaf), adding the remaining fava beans and all the cilantro leaves, plus a drizzle of olive oil. Add red pepper flakes to taste. (See photograph on page 97.)

FOR THE KIBBEH DOUGH
5½oz/1 cup fine bulgur

9oz minced lamb

½ teaspoon ground cinnamon

½ teaspoon ground allspice

freshly ground black pepper
(about ½ teaspoon), to taste

salt (about 1 teaspoon), to taste

FOR THE STUFFING
1 onion, finely chopped

1 tablespoon vegetable oil, plus
extra for frying

5½oz minced lamb

¼ teaspoon ground allspice

¼ teaspoon ground cinnamon

1 teaspoon sumac

1oz/¼ cup pine nuts (or finely
chopped almonds)

a generous pinch of salt

TO SERVE
tahini sauce (see page 67)

lemon wedges

chilli sauce (see page 169),
optional

Lamb Kibbeh

I've eaten these in northern Cyprus many times. In a cobbled market square, women stand under umbrellas in broiling summer heat, shaping the kibbeh and frying them in batches. Piled high and eaten just warm, these crisp, torpedo-shaped shells are filled with a spiced, fragrant filling. Use fine bulgur to form the dough.

First put the bulgur into a bowl and cover with plenty of boiling water. When the bulgur is soft, about 7 minutes, drain well, squeezing out as much water as possible.

To make the stuffing, fry the chopped onion in 1 tablespoon of oil for 8–10 minutes, until completely soft. Add the lamb, spices, pine nuts and salt and cook for 5–10 minutes, until the meat is cooked through. Remove from the heat and set aside, checking the seasoning.

To make the kibbeh dough, use a food processor. Blend the softened bulgur with the raw mince, spices, pepper and salt to form a dough-like consistency. Remove and knead vigorously in a bowl or on a worktop. Place the kibbeh dough in the refrigerator, covered, for 30 minutes to firm up.

Use wet hands to form kibbeh balls the size of a golf ball—roll it well in the palm of your hand to give a smooth surface. Using your thumb, make a hole in the ball to create a deep and even pocket in the kibbeh casing.

Fill the pocket with about 2 teaspoons of cooked lamb stuffing, closing it securely by squeezing the ends together. The kibbeh should be an oval shape with pointed ends. Set the kibbeh on a plate and continue the process until you have used all the dough and filling.

In a non-stick frying pan over a moderate heat, add enough cooking oil to be at least 1¼ inches deep. When the oil is hot, fry the kibbeh in batches until crisp and golden brown all over—about 6–8 minutes. You can deep-fry the kibbeh if you prefer.

Serve hot or even just warm at room temperature, with the tahini sauce and lemon wedges. Chili sauce (see page 169) is good too.

6oz/1 cup spelt, soaked for 1–2 hours and drained

1 bay leaf

2 cloves of garlic, peeled but left whole

salt and freshly ground black pepper

1lb pumpkin (use squash if you prefer), peeled and cut into approx. ¾-inch dice

2 tablespoons extra virgin olive oil

1 onion, finely chopped

1 celery heart, finely chopped

½ teaspoon red pepper flakes

3½oz pancetta or bacon, finely diced (optional)

1 big sprig of fresh rosemary, leaves roughly chopped

5½oz/about 1 cup peeled and chopped chestnuts—roasted fresh or packet is fine

18fl oz–1¾ pints/2¼–4½ cups vegetable or chicken stock

a good-sized bunch of fresh flat-leaf parsley, leaves roughly chopped

TO SERVE
extra virgin olive oil
grated Parmesan or Pecorino cheese, optional

Spelt, Bacon and Pumpkin Rubble with Roasted Chestnuts

Rubble—the clue is in the title. Use farro or barley here if you prefer. You want the chewy grains to work in unison with the other ingredients, with neither grain, pumpkin, bacon nor chestnuts hogging the limelight.

Put the spelt into a pan, cover with plenty of cold water, then add the bay leaf and whole garlic and bring to the boil. Cook until the spelt expands and is just tender, about 25 minutes, adding salt to taste at the end of the cooking time. Drain.

Roast or fry the squash in a little olive oil in a pan until soft and bronzed in places. Depending on the variety and whether it's pan-fried or cooked in the oven (350°F/gas mark 4), the squash should take about 8–15 minutes.

While the spelt is cooking, heat the rest of the olive oil in a large saucepan and cook the onion, celery and red pepper flakes for about 8–10 minutes, until soft, sweet and translucent. Add the pancetta (if using), the roasted squash, the rosemary, chestnuts and cooked spelt and stir well to combine.

Add the stock (you can add as much as little or as much as you like, according to whether you have a rubble or a soupy preference). Bring to a simmer, then cook for 5 minutes for the flavors to meld together.

Stir in the parsley and adjust the seasoning, adding more salt, and freshly ground black pepper as necessary. Serve in bowls, with a little more olive oil drizzled over, perhaps with some grated Parmesan or Pecorino too.

BARLEY (PEARL AND POT)

Often overlooked and viewed as old-fashioned, pearl barley is the most commonly available variety. Quite aside from being extraordinarily cheap, it is a very handy grain, so speedy to cook. As with most grains, barley undergoes a milling process that strips the grain of various layers, altering the nutritional content. The more rigorous the milling process, the less nutritional the product; as such, pearl barley cannot be considered a wholegrain. The softer of the two styles, pearl barley releases its starch into the water as it cooks, which makes it a wonderful ingredient to add to soups and stews to thicken. If you want less viscosity when cooking pearl barley, soak the grains in cold water, giving them a good swishing and sluicing with plenty of fresh water before using them. Alternatively, cook pearl barley separately in water, rinsing it well once cooked before adding to a dish. Boiled in plenty of water, with any froth skimmed during the cooking process, pearl barley can cook in 15–25 minutes.

Pot barley is the grain with its outer husk left intact, and as such rewards its eaters with a more wholesome flavor and toothsome texture. Cooked, it retains its shape much better than pearl. Used as an alternative to wheat grains or spelt in salads, pot barley is a robust and versatile grain to cook with. Boiled in plenty of water, pot barley will cook in approximately 40 minutes.

In Asia, there is an ingredient sold as Chinese barley or, rather more melancholically, Job's tears. While not related to barley, it does look and cook similarly, with a soft, nutty, chewy bite. Unlike barley, it's also gluten-free, so do use this in lieu of barley for these recipes if you prefer.

South-east Asian Stir-fried Barley with Chicken and Cashew Nuts

Barley makes a welcome change from rice in a stir-fry. Enthusiasts of the outlandishly popular Thai dish pad Thai might recognize certain similarities.

4½oz/¾ cup barley, pot or pearl, rinsed

1 tablespoon tamarind paste

1 tablespoon fish sauce

1 teaspoon sugar

1–2 teaspoons red pepper flakes or use fresh chili, to taste

2 tablespoons vegetable oil

2 boneless skinless chicken breasts, cut into bite-sized pieces (or use shrimp if you prefer)

2 cloves of garlic, finely chopped

1 bunch of green onions, finely sliced

5½oz/about 2 cups preserved radish or kimchi (optional, but easy enough to locate), sliced

7oz/2 cups beansprouts (or use peas)

TO GARNISH
1½oz/⅓ cup cashews (or peanuts), roughly chopped

a small bunch of fresh mint, leaves roughly chopped

a small bunch of fresh basil, leaves roughly chopped (Thai basil is best, but not essential)

1 lime, cut into wedges

red pepper flakes or chili sauce fish sauce, to taste (see page 169), to taste

Put the barley into a large saucepan and cover with plenty of cold water (approximately 1 part barley to 3 parts water), then bring to the boil over a high heat. Skim off any froth that surfaces, then reduce the heat and simmer until the grains are tender. Top up the water level if necessary and if the water becomes too starchy. Add salt to taste near the end of the cooking time. The barley is ready when it is tender but still chewy. It may have absorbed all the cooking water—if not, drain well. Pearl will cook much more quickly than pot.

Meanwhile, to make the sauce, combine the tamarind, fish sauce and sugar in a small pan and bring to the boil to dissolve the sugar. Add red pepper flakes to taste and put to one side.

In large pan, ideally a wok, heat 1 tablespoon of oil over a high heat. Add the chicken pieces (or shrimp) and stir-fry for 5–7 minutes, then add the garlic to the pan for the final 2 minutes of cooking time.

Add the cooked barley and stir-fry for an additional 3 minutes, making sure that the chicken is cooked through (cut a piece in half; it should be piping hot throughout). Remove the stir-fried barley and chicken mixture from the pan and keep warm on a plate.

Heat the remaining 1 tablespoon of oil and fry half the cashews for a minute, then add the green onions, preserved radish (or kimchi), if using, and beansprouts (or peas) and fry for 1 minute to combine.

Return the barley-chicken mixture to the wok and stir into the sauce, then stir-fry for 1 minute more and remove from the heat.

Sprinkle the stir-fry with the remaining cashews and all the herbs and serve at the table with the lime wedges, and fish sauce and chili sauce to taste.

Lemon Barley Water

Use pearl barley for this recipe as you want the grain to give up its milky starch to cloud the lemon water. Barley water is an ancient drink that dates back almost 2,000 years. Thought to be health-giving, it was often prescribed to the ill or infirm. Barley water is synonymous now with those fabled tennis lawns in south-west London. It is thirst-quenching and terribly easy to make. Don't discard the cooked barley—you can still use it in lemon-savvy salads or use it instead of brown rice in coconut porridge (see page 81).

Put the barley, water and lemon zest into a saucepan and bring to the boil over a high heat. Skim off any froth that surfaces, then reduce the heat and simmer until the barley is tender—about 15–20 minutes.

Strain the hot barley water into a pitcher and add the sugar to taste, mixing well to dissolve. Add the lemon juice.

Chill in the refrigerator.

To serve, pour into tall glasses with plenty of ice and some fresh mint leaves and lemon slices if desired.

Note: you can also make lemon and ginger barley water with a couple of strips of fresh ginger ¼ inch thick – boil them along with the barley and lemon zest.

2¼oz/about ½ cup pearl barley, rinsed well

2¾ pints/6½ cups cold water

pared zest and juice of 2 lemons—unwaxed is best, if not, washed in hot water and given a scrub (use oranges, Seville too, if you prefer)

2 heaped tablespoons superfine sugar, or to taste

TO SERVE
fresh mint leaves, optional

lemon slices, optional

MAKES ABOUT 3 PINTS

Barley, Radicchio and Ham with an Apple Mustard Dressing

Use only pearl barley for this recipe, as the creamy apple dressing is best suited to the softer cooked grain. The apple juice in the dressing works brilliantly with the crème fraîche and mustard. Sharp, sweet.

Cook the barley as in step 1 on page 102, then drain and place in a serving bowl to cool.

Meanwhile make the dressing by shaking all the ingredients together in a jar.

Toss all the salad ingredients together with the cooked pearl barley and dressing in the bowl. Serve immediately.

FOR THE SALAD
4½oz/about ¾ cup pearl barley, rinsed

1 fennel bulb, trimmed of tough outer leaves and sliced (very thinly)

5½oz/about 1 cup roughly shredded ham, or use shredded ham hock

1 small radicchio, roughly sliced into ribbons

approx. 3½oz/3 cups arugula

a small bunch of fresh flat-leaf parsley, leaves roughly chopped

2 green apples, cored and cut into slices

1¾oz/about ⅓ cup pumpkin seeds

FOR THE DRESSING
4fl oz/½ cup apple juice

2fl oz/¼ cup crème fraîche

2 tablespoons cider vinegar

2 tablespoons Dijon mustard

2 tablespoons grainy mustard

1 shallot, very finely diced (optional, but delicious)

salt and freshly ground black pepper

4 FLOURS

I have a crate that sits on the shelf good and full and squashed with bags of different flours, their tops all rolled down in height according to content. Pale blue stripe, wholesome brown, stout with a shouty promise of All Purpose, paper, cellophane, wholewheat, stoneground, gluten-free, this jumble of half-opened packets full of words and numbers all hold the same promise of alchemy. Mixed with water, milk, yogurt, oil or eggs, leavened sometimes with yeast or a sourdough starter, baking soda, given a handful of seeds, a swirl of honey, a good pinch of salt and so on, the versatility of these pounded grains makes them fundamental to the workings of the pantry. As a raw ingredient, from flour we get: bread, pastry, cakes, batters, dumplings, pancakes, pasta, biscuits, and not least the boiled, fried and baked preparations of coarse-grain flours like polenta, cornmeal and semolina.

On the floor underneath the shelf sits a 35lb sack of bread flour, its steady depletion determined by a firm bread-baking habit. Sometimes I will opt for a 100% white loaf, while at other times I'll mix and match with the different, almost interchangeable, grains of spelt, buckwheat or rye. And sometimes I might prefer to add some wholewheat flour to the mix or go wholewheat all the way. Having an ample selection of flours on your shelf means that you can experiment and find a combination that works best for you and your cooking or baking.

More than anything I enjoy the straightforwardness of using flour to bake bread. Fed yeast or sourdough culture, flour will grow at a pleasing, organic pace. It wants to be bigger than it is. The culture or yeast feeds on the flour, producing carbon dioxide, expediting its growth and eventual transformation. Into a bowl go the flour, leavening agent and water, with salt to be added later. A vigorous stir and left well alone to grow in the half quiet of the house, hours later with the bubble of transformation at full tilt and wet hands to form and fold the dough in on itself, a loaf takes shape. On exit from the oven, here is a perfect loaf with a firm crust the colour of rust, blistered in places, a hairline crack where a gorgeous noisy crackle can escape as the loaf exhales.

If baking bread is a farinaceous mainstay, using alternative flours in my day-to-day cooking unlocks an international food viewpoint. Not all flours respond to gravitational hike. Some work better as a batter to coat, then bake or fry, some fry flat as pancakes, perhaps to stuff and roll then bake again. Some, like polenta or cornmeal, are best of all simply coaxed with liquid to morph in form and serve as sustenance. Wheat-free flours like buckwheat, rye and rice are prized, being good in a wide variety of sweet and savory cooking.

Condensing the flour-based recipes into this one chapter has been a challenge; different flours crop up elsewhere and often. What I'd like best for this collection of recipes is to encourage a confidence to buy and use different flours. And while this selection of flours is by no means absolute, this is an accessible everyday selection. While keen not to demonize wheat (it is a tremendously useful grain for all those tolerant to it), I have also explored flour-based cookery beyond just wheat and white. Understand these flours, get to know their own unique cookability, how each flour responds to different ingredients, and you will feel bolstered by their presence in your pantry.

PANTRY BASICS

WHEAT FLOURS

all-purpose

self-rising

strong white bread

wholewheat/brown

spelt

semolina

PULSE FLOURS

gram (garbanzo bean)

split pea

GRAIN FLOURS

buckwheat

rye

cornmeal or polenta

rice flour

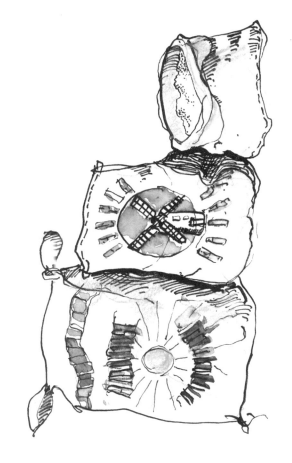

Sourdough Starter

A sourdough starter is a living, breathing pantry staple. A few years ago we asked our good friend Kate to look after our starter for a fortnight; she said she found it more stressful than looking after her daughter's school guinea pig. The sourdough survived (now 10 years old and still going strong), but if I'm honest, my sourdough stripes then still in their infancy, part of me understood Kate's feelings about sourdough and guinea pigs. Sourdough did seem a rather finicky, lengthy method, best left to commercial bakers and not home cooks, for whom a sachet of dried yeast was a fine, reliable option. That was a while ago. I've since got to grips with the method and the maintenance of sourdough and am a convert. That said, I would recommend having a packet of dried yeast in your pantry, as this will give you the best of both baking worlds.

There is a snobbery that comes with sourdough. Some say, the older the origins of the sourdough starter, the better the bread, improving in both sourness and performance with age. Lucky then that serendipity works wonders in sourdough circles. If you use sourdough frequently enough, daily even, the starter will need to be fed every day in order to be super-charged and ready for optimum baking performance. As such, most enthusiasts should have a very merry starter and be willing to give you a small portion to feed up and begin a culture of your own. If you don't happen to know anyone with a culture to breed from, just make your own. Fresh off the press, a newborn starter with no baking pedigree isn't awful; it's all yours and you started it.

To start, take a clean 1¼-pint clip-top Kilner jar (remove the seal for breathing space) and weigh an equal measure (1¾oz/⅜ cup) of bread flour (wholewheat, rye or spelt, organic and top-quality are best) and warm water into the jar, stirring well. Seal and leave in a warm place in your kitchen. Each day, for a week, feed the starter a tablespoon of the same flour and a tablespoon of warm water, stirring well each time. After a week, the mix should be sizeable and have begun to smell sour, with tiny, lively bubbles popping on the surface. In its infancy, the culture will be at its most weak but it should still have the power to leaven bread dough.

Starter husbandry is a fairly undemanding task with very little toil involved. You just need to get your head around the timescales necessary to make, prove and bake a loaf from scratch. If you want to bake sourdough daily, you will need to remove some of the starter and feed the mix with equal flour and water, stirring vigorously. With a healthy sourdough culture, you should need to use all but a few tablespoons of the mix. My baker friend Laura Hart points out that one problem people encounter is an ever-increasing starter, keeping too much back, so you end up with a culture with lots of 'dead' matter in the mix. Feed the sourdough only as much as you need to bake a loaf and be ruthless about not holding too much back, as this will alter the flavor and hamper activity.

The mix should be quite thick and gloopy, with tiny bubbles throughout and especially on the surface; somewhere between the consistency of PVA glue and a very wet bread dough.

If you don't plan on baking for a few days, longer even, you can slow down the ferment by keeping the starter in the refrigerator. Remember, though, the longer it is kept in the refrigerator, the needier and greedier it becomes when you do want to bake with it. On your return to baking, you will need to remove the starter from the refrigerator, keep it somewhere warm and feed it to activate it again. How many feeds you need to give it will depend on the vigor of your culture. I've kept our starter in the refrigerator for over a week, fed it a couple of feeds that same day, and it's been fighting fit to bake with the next day. You can tell whether your starter is ready to bake with by putting a spoon of the mix into a bowl of cold water. If the mix is lively enough to use, the spoonful of culture will float to the top. If it sinks, continue feeding the starter for a few more feeds and test again.

If the worst happens, and your starter is under-used, loses oomph and eventually dies (denatures), you'll know soon enough because any bread you do bake with the starter will be sluggish to prove and the culture will no longer smell deliciously sour and fruity but downright horrid. If this happens, you will have to begin again; it's only flour and water, so what have you got to lose?

Try using sourdough starter in any recipes that call for raising agents, for example, cakes, pikelets or muffins. Sourdough bread also makes the very best breadcrumbs and my pantry has a gaping great hole in it if it's without breadcrumbs, so do blitz up any leftover heels of bread (crusts removed) and store in a jar with a lid.

1lb 2oz/3½ cups strong white
bread flour

10½oz/1⅓ cups warm water

6¾oz/about ⅔ cup sourdough
starter, well fed and lively to bake
with (see pages 114-15)

⅜oz salt

coarse flour—semolina, rice flour
or fine polenta, to bake the loaf

MAKES A 2LB LOAF

White Sourdough Loaf

On the corkboard in my kitchen is a scrap of paper
no bigger than half a postcard in size, and on it are 4
measurements, the words 'wet hands' and 2 timings.
Wild yeasts (the sourdough culture), flour, water and
salt; making bread with a sourdough starter is baking at
its most rewarding and is certainly the most inexpensive
way to get your hands on a loaf of sourdough.

The dough will be very wet, but use wet hands and,
with a bit of practice, you'll soon get the hang of it.
The dough first takes shape by vigorous mixing and,
over time, as the dough knits together (autolyzes), form
is given to the loaf by both the action of gently folding
the dough in on itself to create a smooth surface tension
and the leavening of the dough as it proves.

NOTE ON YOUR STARTER

If your starter is kept at room temperature, feed it the
day before you bake. If it's refrigerated you might need
to give it a morning and night feed the day before you
want to bake with it. If your starter has formed a dark
liquid on the top, pour this off. This liquid shows the
starter is exhausted (literally, so hungry it has begun
to eat itself) and needs to be fed back to fighting form.
If you are baking daily and your starter is at full tilt,
use the portion you remove to bake with and replace
what you take with new flour and water. If your starter
needs feeding to bake with in the first place, discard
all but a few tablespoons of the starter, feeding only
what remains in the jar. To do this, replace what you
have discarded with an equal measure of new flour and
warm water—you need to add enough in order to have
the required portion to bake with, i.e. 6¾oz as per this
recipe. There is no need to weigh this, you can do it by
eye, and you will soon get the hang of it. Stir vigorously.

SOURDOUGH: FIRST PROVE

Use digital kitchen scales to weigh everything, including liquid. Put all the ingredients except the salt and the coarse flour for baking into a large mixing bowl and mix together with a large metal spoon. Make sure all the flour is mixed into the liquid. The dough will look rough and not be smooth at all, but it should be cohesive.

Cover and let the dough rest for about 30 minutes to autolyze. The dough will not yet have begun to prove, but this process is crucial for the flour to hydrate completely and for the gluten to start to strengthen. Adding the salt before this step is complete will inhibit the desired gluten development.

After this time, add the salt to the dough and, using wet hands, lift and fold the dough, mixing the salt through.

Cover the bowl with plastic wrap or (top tip here) a clear, elasticated shower cap. Leave it somewhere warmish to rise. This first rise is sometimes called the 'bulk fermentation' and can take anywhere between 3 and 12 hours, depending on the ambient temperature and the strength of the starter. The dough needs to expand to about 1½ times its original size. During this period, using wet hands, you can occasionally tuck the sides under the round of dough again, folding it round on itself. This isn't vital, but helps the dough keep its shape after the fermentation process.

SOURDOUGH: 2ND PROVE AND SHAPING

Lightly flour a work surface. The dough will be less wet and easier to work with from now on. Remove it from the bowl, and scrape it on to the floured surface. Gather the round of dough and fold it approximately 4 times in on itself, retaining the round shape. Turn the dough over and place it seam side down. Using your hands, gently cup the sides of the dough and rotate until you have a nice round, tight loaf shape.

Lay a clean cotton or linen dish towel (not a fluffy one) on the table and generously dust with semolina, fine polenta or rice flour to stop the dough sticking. Place the shaped dough on it, this time seam side up. Fold up the corners, place in a bowl or colander to hold the shape and cover with plastic wrap or a shower cap. I use a colander with a handle to make it easier to flip the loaf out and over when ready to bake, but you could use a proving basket if you have one. Leave for 1 hour, or until almost doubled in size, before baking.

BAKING THE SOURDOUGH

I use the Dutch oven method to bake my sourdough at home. Housed in the hot pot, the loaf has nowhere else to go but up and the finished loaf will have a good uniform shape with an incredible crust. Using this method, I find, can ape professionally baked sourdough loaves baked on the stone in fearsomely hot bread ovens. You will need either a plain cast-iron 5¼-pint casserole pot with a cast-iron lid, or a traditional and similar-sized Dutch oven pan. Anything but 100% cast-iron risks cracking with heat shock.

Preheat your oven to 450°F/gas mark 8, or as hot as possible.

Place your pot in the very hot oven for 5 minutes to heat through.

Remove the hot pot from the oven and quickly and carefully turn the bread out into the pot. It should come away from the dish towel; if not, give it a gentle prod.

With the dough in the pot and before the lid is put on and the pot is returned to the oven, use a serrated knife, very sharp knife or even a pair of scissors to slash the loaf. Three horizontal stripes or an approximate square are both good, with each incision 1¼ inches or so long and ½ inch deep. The slash allows the steam to escape and the dough to expand.

Put the lid on and place the pot in the hot oven, reducing the temperature to 400°F/gas mark 6. Bake for 25 minutes with the lid on.

After this time, remove the lid from the pot and bake uncovered for an additional 12–15 minutes, or until the loaf is a deep, golden brown with a firm crust.

If you have one, you can use a temperature probe to measure the internal temperature of the loaf. It is ready if the thermometer reads 230°F. Alternatively, remove the loaf from the pot and give it a good tap on the bottom. It will sound hollow if it's ready.

Cool on a wire rack for at least 45 minutes before cutting.

CHECKLIST

- Feed the starter
- Check the starter is ready
- Mix dough/autolyze
- Add salt
- Bulk fermentation (first rise) (time to add additional flavors here)—a few folds during this stage are beneficial
- Shape loaf
- Second rise—in cloth in a basket, colander or baking receptacle
- Tip shaped loaf into hot pot
- Cut or slash
- Lid
- Bake
- Rest

VARIATION: MUESLI BREAD SOURDOUGH

This is really easy and makes a brilliant breakfast loaf.

Just add about 3oz/1 cup of muesli to the sourdough dough during the first (bulk) fermentation. Proceed as described on previous pages.

SOURDOUGH BAKING PROCESS IN 24 HOURS

Night before: remove the starter from the refrigerator, pour off any clear or grey liquid collected on the top, remove all but a few tablespoons of the starter to make room to feed the sourdough, and use enough new flour and warm water to feed the mix in order to have the required portion to bake with. Mix well—you want it quite thick. Leave out overnight.

Morning: to check the starter is ready, drop a spoonful in a glass of water—it should float to the top. Make the dough and leave to bulk ferment, 1st prove.

Afternoon or evening: shape the dough ready for the second rise.

Bake.

FINAL FINAL NOTE

The more you use sourdough and get to grips with it in baking, the more confident you will become with it as a process. Soon enough you will get to know the qualities (personality!) of your starter and understand better its productivity on, say, a hot day or if you have used it in an overnight prove in the cool of a winter's kitchen. Confidence is in the timing of the whole process; speeding up the rise with warmer water or slowing down the rise of a loaf in the refrigerator overnight while you sleep. It is not a recipe but an understanding. Good luck and all power to your sourdough.

9oz sourdough dough
(¼ quantity of sourdough
loaf dough, page 116)

2 teaspoons fennel seeds

½ teaspoon salt

2 tablespoons superfine sugar

3 tablespoons olive oil

1 egg white, beaten

MAKES 10

Olive Oil Tortas

These crackers, biscuits, call them what you will, are hideously expensive to buy in the shops. Make your own—they are a doddle. Make your usual measure of sourdough dough: use three-quarters to make a slightly smaller loaf, and use the remaining quarter to make these beautiful slim, crisp fennel and olive oil-scented tortas.

When the dough has autolyzed (see sourdough, page 117), add the fennel seeds, salt and half the sugar, then mix in the olive oil.

Allow to bulk ferment as in the sourdough bread method on page 117.

When ready to bake, preheat the oven to 425°F/gas mark 7 and lightly oil a large baking sheet lined with baking parchment.

Lightly flour your work surface and your rolling pin with flour. Divide the dough into 10 equal-sized balls, then roll out each ball until it's almost translucent and about 4 inches in diameter. Place each torta on the lined baking sheet and lightly brush with beaten egg white, then sprinkle with the remaining sugar (you might need to do this in batches).

Bake for 8–10 minutes, or until golden and crisp, watching carefully as they can burn quickly.

Transfer the tortas to wire racks to cool before serving. Best eaten the day they are baked.

Sourdough Soup

Thanks to Tom and Anna Herbert of the UK's Hobbs House Bakery, who made this delicious lunch for me after a mammoth sourdough bake-off last summer in their bright bakery classroom. The use of the starter in the soup was an absolute revelation and one that makes brilliant use of any excess starter removed, if you don't use it to bake bread with and don't want to just throw it away to make room to feed the sourdough. Not only does it thicken the soup, but it also gives wonderful fruity sour notes to this earthy, punchy soup. Love it.

SERVES 4–6

2–3 tablespoons olive oil

2 onions, diced

7oz/1 cup garbanzo beans, soaked overnight and cooked, or use 1 x 14oz can of garbanzo beans, rinsed and drained

5oz/¾ cup red lentils, rinsed

1 x 14oz can of tomatoes

4 celery stalks, sliced or diced

1 tablespoon tomato paste

1 teaspoon ground ginger

2 cinnamon sticks

1 teaspoon ground turmeric

1¾ pints/4½ cups chicken or vegetable stock, hot (use boiling water if you like)

10½oz/about 1 cup sourdough starter (see page 114)

salt and freshly ground black pepper

a small bunch of fresh cilantro, leaves roughly chopped

a small bunch of fresh flat-leaf parsley, leaves roughly chopped

juice of 1 lemon

Put the oil into a heavy-bottomed saucepan over a moderate heat, add the onions and cook until completely soft, about 8–10 minutes.

Add the garbanzo beans, lentils, tomatoes and celery along with the tomato paste and the spices, and cook for a further 5 minutes.

Add the hot stock and bring to the boil.

Add approximately 2 cupfuls of the hot soup to the sourdough starter and stir in a bowl to combine.

Add the sourdough mix back to the soup and stir thoroughly over a moderate heat—no need to boil, just stir until thickened nicely.

Check the seasoning of the soup, adding a little more hot stock or water if it has become too thick.

Remove the cinnamon sticks, and a few spoonfuls of chickpeas for serving, then blend the soup.

Serve immediately, with some chopped herbs, a few chickpeas, a squeeze of lemon and a hunk of sourdough on the side.

1lb 2oz/3½ cups strong white
bread flour

¼oz sachet of dried yeast

12½fl oz/just over 1½ cups warm
water

1 teaspoon salt

coarse flour—semolina, rice flour
or fine polenta, to bake the loaf

MAKES A 2LB LOAF

White Yeasted Loaf
(Dutch oven method)

**From my previous book, but included here as an option
when making some of these recipes requiring bread,
should you not be using sourdough. A wet dough, this
is a no-knead bread recipe. Yeast is an ally in baking
should you want to bake in a shorter format than
sourdough affords. As in sourdough baking, the Dutch
oven method is great if you want a round loaf with the
characteristic crust.**

Put the flour and yeast into a large mixing bowl.

Make a well in the center and pour in the water, mixing
very well to combine. The mix will feel wet. Vigorously
move the dough around the bowl with a spoon or with
wet hands for about 45 seconds to 1 minute.

Cover the bowl with plastic wrap or a plastic shower cap
and put aside somewhere warm for 30 minutes.

After this time, add the salt to the dough, giving it a
good mix with a spoon or wet hands. Leave the dough
covered in the bowl until not quite doubled in size.

Lightly flour your work surface. The dough will be
less wet and easier to work with from now on. Remove
the dough from the bowl, and scrape it on to the
floured surface. Gather the round of dough and fold
it approximately 4 times in on itself, retaining the round
shape. Turn the dough over and place it seam side
down. Using your hands, gently cup the sides of the
dough and rotate until you have a nice round, tight
loaf shape.

Spread a clean cotton or linen dish towel (not a fluffy
one) on the table and generously dust it with semolina,
fine polenta or rice flour to stop the dough sticking.
Place the shaped dough on it, this time seam side up.
Fold up the corners and place in a bowl or colander to
hold the shape and cover with plastic wrap or a shower
cap. I use a colander with a handle to make it easier
to flip the loaf out and over when ready to bake—you
could use a bread proving basket if you have one.

Ideally, you want the loaf to be about a third off fully doubled in size when it is ready to bake. This way, the loaf will still have some unused energy to use up as it hits the heat of the oven. The surface of the dough should be smooth and cohesive, with no rips or tears.

Preheat your oven to 450°F/gas mark 8, or as hot as possible.

Place your pot in the very hot oven for 5 minutes to heat through.

Remove the hot pot from the oven and quickly and carefully turn the bread into it. It should come away from the dish towel; if not, give it a good prod.

With the dough in the pot and before the lid is put on and the pot is returned to the oven, use a serrated knife, very sharp knife or even a pair of scissors to slash the loaf—3 horizontal stripes or an approximate square are both good, with each incision 1¼ inches or so long and ½ inch deep. The slash allows the steam to escape and the dough to expand.

Put the lid on and place the pot in the hot oven, reducing the temperature to 400°F/gas mark 6. Bake for 25 minutes with the lid on.

After this time, remove the lid and bake uncovered for an additional 12–15 minutes, or until the loaf is a deep, golden brown with a firm crust.

If you have one, you can use a temperature probe to measure the internal temperature of the loaf. It is ready if the thermometer reads 203°F. Alternatively, remove the loaf from the pot and give it a good tap on the bottom. It will sound hollow if it's ready.

Cool on a wire rack before cutting.

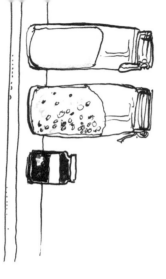

Three-Seed Wholewheat Loaf

This is a variation on the white yeasted loaf (see pages 128–9). Sourdough behaves differently with brown or wholewheat flour, so if you're after a brown sourdough, by all means read up elsewhere. I've opted to use yeast in this seeded loaf.

Follow the method and cooking times given on pages 128–9, adding the seeds to the flour when you add the yeast and water.

14oz/3½ cups wholewheat or strong brown bread flour

3½oz/just under 1 cup strong white bread flour

¼oz sachet of dried yeast

12½fl oz/just over 1½ cups cold water

approx. 3oz/½ cup seeds, a combination or solo: pumpkin, sunflower, sesame or linseed (omit for plain loaf)

1 teaspoon salt

MAKES A 2LB LOAF

Sausage and Fennel Seed Sourdough Focaccia

Sausage and fennel is a favorite combination. Cooked here on top of bread dough laced with olive oil, thirsty from the heat of the oven, I think this focaccia gives good pizza a run for its money.

Spread the proven dough to fit an approximately 10 x 14 inch deep oven tray. Cover it with plastic wrap and allow to rise again for about 45 minutes.

While you're waiting for the focaccia to prove, prepare the topping. Heat 2 tablespoons of olive oil in a large pan over a medium heat, then add the potatoes and fennel to the pan and cook for around for 5 minutes, just until they are slightly softened. Add the seeds and continue to cook for a further minute or two. Leave to cool, then add the squeezed-out sausage meat, mixing it in among the fennel and potato mix, leaving in the odd big chunk here and there.

Preheat the oven to 400°F/gas mark 6.

Once the focaccia has risen sufficiently, 'dimple' the dough using well-oiled fingertips, digging deeply enough to give good indentation but not so much as to go through the dough and into the tray. Drizzle the remaining olive oil over the top of the dough. Spread the potato and sausage mix, along with the rosemary and the salt, evenly over the top of the focaccia.

Put the tray into the oven and bake the focaccia for about 25 minutes, until golden brown and with a good crust. It should sound hollow when tapped underneath or have an internal temperature of 203°F if you use a digital thermometer.

Remove the tray from the oven and drizzle the hot focaccia with a little extra olive oil, about a good tablespoon's worth.

Leave to cool for 10 minutes on a wire rack before serving.

1 x quantity of sourdough (see page 116) after bulk fermentation or yeasted bread dough (see page 128) after the first prove and before you would shape it into a round

FOR THE TOPPING
4 tablespoons olive oil, plus extra to drizzle on the cooked loaf

3½oz new potatoes, thinly sliced, no thicker than ⅛ inch

½ a fennel bulb, trimmed of tough outer leaves and thinly sliced

1–2 teaspoons crushed fennel seed

5¼oz sausage, casings removed, meat squished out (approx. 2 sausages' worth)

2 sprigs of fresh rosemary, leaves chopped

½ teaspoon salt, coarse or flaky

Impanata

A Sicilian-style pie made with a bread dough and stuffed full with broccoli, herbs and ricotta. Make this and watch as your guests beam at the wonder that is, dare I even say it, stuffed crust. Use cooked and drained spinach or chard in lieu of the broccoli, if you like.

Line a baking sheet with baking parchment.

Cook the broccoli and garlic in plenty of boiling salted water until soft, then drain well and leave to cool.

In a mixing bowl combine the cooked broccoli, cooked onion, ricotta, egg, herbs, spices, Parmesan and finally salt and pepper to taste.

Divide the proved dough in half and turn it out on to an oiled work surface.

Working with one half at a time, place the dough on a piece of parchment, or on a lightly greased baking sheet. Pat and push it into a circle about ½ inch thick, a bit like a pizza round.

Spread one round with the broccoli filling, leaving a 1¼ inch border. Place the other round on top, crimping and pressing the edges together to seal.

Cut 4 or 5 slits in the top (scissors are good for this), to allow steam to escape, and brush with olive oil.

Gently place the impanata on the prepared baking sheet, lifting it carefully. Let it rest, uncovered, for 30 minutes, while you preheat the oven to 425°F/gas mark 7.

Bake for 20–30 minutes, until golden brown with a firm crust.

Remove from the oven and cool for at least 5–10 minutes before slicing and serving.

7oz broccoli, broken into smaller florets

4 cloves of garlic, peeled and left whole

1 onion, finely diced and cooked in olive oil or butter until soft and translucent (8–10 minutes)

4½oz/1¼ cups ricotta, cottage cheese or quark

1 egg, beaten

a small bunch of fresh herbs: oregano, dill or flat-leaf parsley, leaves finely chopped

1 teaspoon crushed fennel seeds

1 tablespoon dried oregano

¼ teaspoon red pepper flakes (optional)

1½oz/½ cup freshly grated Parmesan cheese

salt and freshly ground black pepper

½ quantity sourdough dough, after bulk fermentation (see page 116), or ½ quantity of yeasted white dough (see page 128) after the first prove and before you shape it into a round

Soft Pretzel Sticks

These soft pretzels are delicious. The hefty measure of baking soda in the water as you boil the pretzels is crucial to the spontaneous burst in height that the dough achieves in the boiling process. Best eaten still warm, swooped through softened butter and some of that dayglo hotdog mustard.

Mix and knead the brown sugar, water, oil, flour and yeast by hand or in a mixer to make a cohesive, fairly smooth dough. It should be slightly sticky—if it seems dry, knead in an additional tablespoon or two of water. Cover and rest for 10 minutes.

Add a pinch of salt and fold the dough a couple of times, then cover and let it rest for 45 minutes.

Turn the dough out on to a lightly floured work surface, fold it over a few times to gently deflate it, then divide it into 12 pieces. Use a bit of flour to roll each piece of dough into an 8-inch rope, then place on an oiled baking tray and leave for 30 minutes, uncovered.

Preheat the oven to 425°F/gas mark 7.

Meanwhile, bring a large pan of water to the boil. Carefully add the baking soda to the boiling water —it will bubble up.

Gently remove the pretzels from the baking tray and drop them into the boiling water, 3 or 4 at a time. Simmer for about 30 seconds, then turn them and simmer for an additional 30 seconds. Remove with a slotted spoon and place on a clean dish towel to dry, then return to the baking tray. Repeat with the remaining pretzels, boiling in batches.

Brush the pretzels with the egg wash and sprinkle with salt and sesame or poppy seeds, if using. Bake until richly browned, about 12–15 minutes.

When you remove the pretzels from the oven, brush with the melted butter and serve warm with mustard and additional softened, room temperature butter.

1¾oz/¼ cup light brown sugar

8½oz/1 cup water

2 tablespoons vegetable oil

11¼oz/2½ cups strong white bread flour, plus extra for kneading (or substitute 3oz/about ½ cup of the white flour with dark rye for a more complex pretzel flavor)

¼oz sachet of dried yeast

flaky or coarse sea salt

1¾oz/4 level tablespoons baking soda

1 egg, beaten with 1 tablespoon water

seeds to top—sesame or poppy (optional)

melted butter, about 2 tablespoons

yellow mustard and softened, room temperature butter, to serve

MAKES 12

Chijimi

Korean-style pancake batter, fried with thinly cut vegetables and the mighty, all-important refrigerator staple that is kimchi (pickled cabbage). Served here with a dipping sauce, these brilliant pancakes can be small and individual or cooked large and chopped into bite-sized pieces to plunge into the dipping sauce.

In a large bowl, mix the flour, a big pinch of salt and the sesame seeds. Slowly mix in 9fl oz/1 cup of water, the egg and the sesame oil, making sure there are no lumps.

Add the kimchi and vegetables to the batter and mix well.

In a separate bowl, mix the dipping sauce ingredients, adding chili to taste.

Heat enough oil to cover the base of a large frying pan placed over a medium heat, and pour in the batter to cover the base of the pan. Cook for 2–3 minutes, or until the edges and underside have begun to crisp up. Flip over and cook for another 2 minutes.

Cut into bite-sized pieces and serve with the dipping sauce.

FOR THE PANCAKES
7oz/1½ cups all-purpose flour

salt

1 tablespoon sesame seeds

1 egg, beaten

1 tablespoon sesame oil

3½–5½oz/about 1½–2 cups shredded kimchi (according to taste)

7oz/about 3 cups very finely sliced vegetables: green onions, chives, beansprouts (no need to slice these), carrots, cabbage, spinach, red onion, etc.

vegetable oil, for frying

FOR THE DIPPING SAUCE
2 tablespoons soy sauce

1 tablespoon vinegar

1 teaspoon sugar

1 tablespoon sesame seeds

1 teaspoon sesame oil

a pinch of chilli powder or chilli oil (see page 169), to taste

MAKES 1 BIG PANCAKE, TO CUT INTO SMALLER TRIANGLES

Semolina Gnocchi

1¾ pints/4½ cups milk

7oz/1⅔ cups fine semolina

3½oz/1⅓ cups freshly grated Parmesan cheese, plus extra to serve

salt and freshly ground black pepper

2 egg yolks

3½oz/just under ½ cup butter

Semolina gnocchi are a better bet than the potentially gluey potato variety. Crucial to the gnocchi holding together when baked is the cooking time on the hob, and beating continuously as the mixture cooks. Serve with brown sage butter or any of the pasta sauces on pages 22–34.

Heat the milk in a saucepan over a medium heat until it is just before the boiling point. Turn the heat down to low, and very slowly start pouring in the semolina in a steady stream, beating it constantly with a whisk. Keep beating until it becomes heavy and starts sticking to the whisk, about 10 minutes. Take off the heat.

Stir in two-thirds of the Parmesan, a good pinch of salt, the yolks and half the butter. Stir quickly until all the ingredients are mixed.

Line a flat baking tray with baking parchment and dampen it slightly with some cold water. Spread the hot semolina mix out over the parchment, smoothing it out to a thickness of roughly ⅝ inch. Leave to cool completely for at least 30 minutes.

Preheat the oven to 400°F/gas mark 6 and butter a large baking dish generously. Use a wet knife to cut the cooled semolina into approximately 3-inch squares. Transfer the gnocchi to the dish, overlapping them slightly, then dot with the remaining butter, sprinkle over the remaining Parmesan and add a grind of pepper. Place in the oven for 10–15 minutes, or until a light golden crust has formed and the gnocchi are turning golden brown.

Remove from the oven and serve with the sage butter.

Sage Butter

1¾oz/¼ cup butter

approx. 6–8 fresh sage leaves

juice of ½ a lemon

Put the butter and sage leaves into a small pan and cook over a moderate heat, stirring and scraping until it begins to foam and the sediment starts to fall away and turn golden brown. Add the lemon juice to stop the butter from turning too brown and cooking any more. Pour the butter into a bowl and keep somewhere warm until ready to use.

Semolina and Date Bars

These are loosely based on the Lebanese ma'amoul biscuits, which use traditional wooden molds to shape the dough. I've used traditional wooden molds to shape the dough. I've rolled the biscuit dough and cut it flat, rolling it round the filling and making more of a log or a bar than a cookie or a biscuit. I've also added tahini, which complements the sweet, sticky date filling.

2¾oz/½ cup fine semolina

7oz/just under 2 cups self-rising flour, plus extra for rolling (or use all-purpose flour with ½ teaspoon baking powder)

a pinch of salt

3½oz/½ cup ground almonds

1¾oz/¼ cup superfine sugar

1¾oz/¼ cup unsalted butter

1¾oz/¼ cup tahini (or use more butter)

2 tablespoons rose water or orange blossom water

1 egg, beaten

3 tablespoons sesame seeds

superfine or confectioners' sugar, to dust

FOR THE DATE FILLING

1lb 2oz/about 2½ cups soft dates or figs

3½oz/½ cup unsalted butter, cubed

1 teaspoon ground cinnamon

¼ teaspoon ground cardamom

MAKES ABOUT 16

Mix the semolina, flour, salt, almonds and sugar in a bowl. Gently melt the butter, add the tahini and rose water, then pour this into the bowl and rub through with your fingers until it looks a bit like wet sand (alternatively, you can carefully pulse the mix in a food processor).

Add the egg and gently form into a ball, then cover and leave for 1 hour so the semolina swells and softens.

Make the date filling by blending the dates with the butter and spices until smooth. Chill the mix in the refrigerator to firm up, 30 minutes to 1 hour.

Lightly flour a work surface and also your rolling pin, and roll out the dough ⅕ inch thick to a strip about 16 inches long and 8 inches wide. Cut this into four 4 x 8-inch strips.

Divide the filling into four and form each piece into a 8 inch long sausage-shaped piece. Place one along the center of each piece of dough. Roll the dough around the filling, then crimp or pinch tightly along the edge to seal each shape.

Roll the logs through the sesame seeds and slice each into four. Place on a baking tray.

Heat the oven to 400°F/gas mark 6 and bake the rolls for about 15–20 minutes, until the edges and top turn golden brown.

As soon as they're out of the oven, sprinkle them with the superfine or confectioners' sugar and cool on a wire rack.

Spelt and Walnut Cake

The ancestor of modern milled wheat flour, white or wholewheat spelt is enormously useful in various kinds of baking. With a delicious nutty flavor and a good crumbly texture when used in baked goods, spelt has less gluten than mass-produced wheat, making it easier on the digestive tract for some people. With the walnuts, the characteristics of spelt excel in this recipe.

Preheat the oven to 350°F/gas mark 4 and line an 8-inch cake tin.

Put the dates and the measure of tea or water into a small saucepan and bring to the boil.

Remove from the heat and blend, then stir in the baking soda and allow the mixture to cool.

In a bowl beat together the eggs and sugar until light and fluffy, then mix in the oil, spelt flour, baking powder and walnuts. Finally add the blended date mixture and mix well.

Pour the mixture into the prepared cake tin and bake for 50–60 minutes, until golden brown, firm to touch and a skewer inserted into the center of the cake comes out clean.

Remove from the oven and leave to cool on a wire rack before cutting into slices and serving.

5½oz/about 1 cup pitted dates

5fl oz/⅝ cup freshly brewed tea (use boiling water if you prefer)

½ teaspoon baking soda

3 eggs

3½oz/½ cup soft brown sugar

5fl oz/⅝ cup sunflower oil

7oz/just under 2 cups spelt flour

2 teaspoons baking powder

2¾oz/¾ cup walnuts, chopped

spelt flakes or rolled oats, to top and add through

MAKES 1 X 8-INCH CAKE

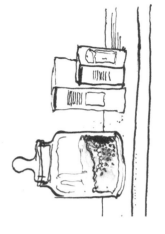

PULSE FLOURS

Pakora (North India) or Bhaji (South India)

Gram flour is made from garbanzo beans and is gluten-free. It is readily available in Indian grocery shops and bigger supermarkets. My pantry is never without it. Gram flour is one of the most versatile flours I use and one I rely on heavily in my home cooking. Common in Indian, Bangladeshi, Pakistani and Nepali recipes, it is also used extensively in southern European cooking. It is a ridiculously inexpensive and brilliant ingredient.

CHOOSE 3 OF THE FOLLOWING:

- 1 medium onion, thinly sliced
- 1 green bell pepper, thinly sliced
- 1 large carrot, cut into short matchsticks or coarsely grated
- 1 medium potato, cut into short matchsticks or coarsely grated
- ¼ head of cauliflower, broken into small florets
- handful of cilantro leaves, roughly chopped
- 3 green or red chili peppers, thinly sliced
- 1 eggplant, thinly sliced then cut into matchsticks
- 2 handfuls of spinach, thinly sliced into ribbons
- ¼ cabbage, thinly sliced into ribbons

neutral oil, for shallow frying (sunflower, vegetable, groundnut)
½ teaspoon salt
2 teaspoons masala or curry powder, plus extra to serve
1 teaspoon ground turmeric
1 teaspoon cumin seeds
½ teaspoon red pepper flakes (optional—or more to taste)
3½oz/¾ cup gram flour

Prepare your choice of vegetables (see left).

Heat up the oil in a large pan or wok to a medium heat, deep enough to shallow fry the vegetables.

Sprinkle the salt and spices into a large mixing bowl and sift in the gram flour. Add a small amount of water (about 4fl oz/½ cup in total), a little at a time, to make a thick batter that will coat all the vegetables. Add the vegetables and mix well. Do not leave the batter and vegetable mixture for too long before cooking.

Test your oil is hot enough by dropping a little batter into the oil. If it browns and rises immediately, it is ready. Very carefully drop spoonfuls of the mixture into the oil and fry until golden brown, turning them over in the boiling oil if necessary with a slotted spoon.

Work in batches, being careful to not overcrowd the pan.

Once golden brown and crisp, remove from the oil and set aside on some kitchen paper, sprinkled with a bit more garam masala or curry powder and a little extra salt if you like.

Serve with jarred Indian pickles, seasoned yogurt and lime wedges.

Socca or Farinata

Socca, as it is known in the south of France, or farinata, as it's called in Italy, specifically in Liguria, is a popular street food. It is baked flat like a pancake and cut into wedges.

Southern French version:
Socca with artichokes and rosemary

Preheat the oven to 400°F/gas mark 6.

In a bowl, mix the water with the gram flour, olive oil and salt. Cover and let stand for about an hour at room temperature.

When ready to cook, heat a well-seasoned 12-inch cast-iron ovenproof frying pan/skillet over a high heat.

When very hot, add a good slug of olive oil, about 2 tablespoons should do, and add the drained artichokes. Distribute them evenly over the surface of the pan, letting them sizzle over a high heat for 20 seconds or so.

Add the chopped rosemary to the batter and pour it into the pan over a continued high heat. Let it stay over the heat for a minute to crisp on the bottom.

Put the pan into the oven and cook for 12–15 minutes, until firm to touch and golden brown and crisp in places.

Remove from the oven and serve with lemon wedges, and a liberal seasoning of salt and pepper.

1lb/just under 2 cups warm water

just under 2 cups gram flour

½ teaspoon sea salt

3 tablespoons olive oil, plus extra to cook

1 x 14oz can of artichoke hearts, drained

a large sprig of fresh rosemary, leaves finely chopped

TO SERVE
lemon wedges

salt and freshly ground black pepper

MAKES 1 THICK PANCAKE,
TO SERVE 4

1 quantity of batter, (see page 141)

olive oil, to cook

1 red onion, sliced into rounds

2 tablespoons freshly ground
black pepper

1 lemon, halved, to serve

salt

MAKES 2 SLIGHTLY THINNER
PANCAKES

Ligurian Farinata with Red Onion and Lots of Black Pepper

Prepare the batter as on page 141 and divide the mix in two, to make two thinner pancakes.

When ready to cook, heat a well-seasoned 12-inch cast-iron frying pan to very hot.

Add about 2–3 tablespoons of olive oil, and pour half the batter into the pan. Quickly distribute half the onion rings into the batter and continue to fry over a moderate to high heat for 2–3 minutes. Add half the black pepper to the batter as it cooks.

Check to see that the underside is nicely crisped, then quickly flip the farinata over and cook on the other side for a further 2–3 minutes, until the sides are crisp and the onion beneath has softened and coloured considerably.

Remove from the heat and serve immediately, with plenty of lemon squeezed over the farinata and salt to taste. Repeat with the remaining batter, onions and pepper to make the second one while you eat the first piping hot.

GRAIN FLOURS

Buckwheat Crespelle with Three Fillings

Crespelle are Italian savory pancakes, fried thinly and stuffed with various ingredients to bake again. In Brittany and Belgium, buckwheat flour is the common flour used when making pancakes, lending a nutty flavor, more complex than wheat. Related to the rhubarb plant, buckwheat seeds are milled like wheat grains and make for a dark, freckled flour with a lovely sweet/sour taste. Make these pancakes and experiment with the different fillings on these pages.

FOR THE PANCAKES
5½oz/1 cup buckwheat flour

3 eggs, beaten

9fl oz/1 cup milk

¾oz/just over 1 tablespoon butter, melted and cooled, plus extra to cook

For the pancakes (crespelle), place the flour in a bowl. Use a whisk to stir in the eggs and milk until well combined and smooth. Slowly mix in the melted butter and set aside for 10 minutes. Stir in enough water to give the mixture the consistency of pouring cream, about 2fl oz/¼ cup.

Heat an approximately 8-inch non-stick frying pan over a medium heat. Add a piece of butter and swirl to coat.

Add about 1¾fl oz/3½ tablespoons of the batter and tilt the pan to cover the base. Cook for 1–2 minutes, or until the edges start to curl. Turn over and cook for a further 1–2 minutes, or until golden. Transfer to a plate and cover with a clean dish towel. Repeat with the remaining batter, to make about 12 crespelle.

Asparagus/ham

2–3 bunches of asparagus, about 15–20 spears

about 10 slices of prosciutto or thinly sliced ham (smoked is nice)

butter or olive oil

1 clove of garlic

freshly grated Parmesan cheese, to serve

Cook the asparagus in boiling water for about 4–5 minutes, until tender. Wrap the asparagus in pairs with the ham, tearing it into pieces if necessary.

Wrap each ham-wrapped asparagus pair in a pancake and lay them side by side snugly in a greased (butter or olive oil) baking dish that has been rubbed with garlic.

This can be topped with cream, béchamel or fried mushrooms in cream and baked at about 350°F/gas mark 4 for about 25 minutes. Or the crespelle can just be dotted with butter and grated with Parmesan as it comes out to serve.

Spinach/ricotta

Mix the spinach, ricotta, cheese and nutmeg together and season with salt and pepper.

Fill the pancakes and roll them up, laying them side by side snugly in a greased (butter or olive oil) baking dish that has been rubbed with garlic.

This can be topped with cream, béchamel or tomato sauce and baked at about 350°F/gas mark 4 for about 25 minutes. Or the crespelle can just be dotted with a little butter and warmed through in the oven with plenty of grated Parmesan as it comes out to serve.

9oz/about 1 cup thawed frozen or cooked spinach, squeezed dry

9oz/just over 1 cup ricotta

3½oz/1⅓ cups freshly grated Parmesan or Pecorino cheese

nutmeg, about ¼, freshly grated—or more to taste

salt and freshly ground black pepper

butter or olive oil

1 clove of garlic

Mushroom/potato

Melt 1 tablespoon of butter in a medium pan and add the onion, then cover and cook over a low heat for 10 minutes, until soft and lightly golden. Uncover, add the chopped garlic and cook for 1 minute more. Add the potatoes and then add them to the pan with the cream and some seasoning. Simmer gently for 15–20 minutes, stirring carefully every now and then until the potatoes are tender. (Be careful they don't catch on the bottom of the pan.)

Heat the remaining butter in a frying pan, add the mushrooms and fry for 3 minutes until tender, and season lightly. Stir into the potatoes, add the cheese and check the seasoning.

Fill each pancake with the mix and lay them side by side snugly in a buttered baking dish that has been rubbed with garlic.

This can be topped with cream or béchamel and baked at about 350°F/gas mark 4 for about 25 minutes. Or the crespelle can be dotted with a little butter and warmed through in the oven to serve.

1oz/2 tablespoons butter, plus extra for the dish and to bake

1 small onion, finely chopped

1 clove of garlic, chopped, plus 1 clove for the dish

7oz small waxy potatoes, peeled and sliced ¼ inch thick

5fl oz/¾ cup heavy cream

3½oz chestnut mushrooms, halved and thinly sliced

salt and freshly ground black pepper

1¾oz/½ cup grated hard, mature cheese such as Gruyère or Cheddar

CORNMEAL

Cornmeal is made by grinding dried corn kernels into one of three textures: fine, medium or coarse. Cooked over a low heat with water or sometimes milk, it is a staple dish known in Italy as polenta and in America as grits. I am not a fan of the par-cooked/quick-cooked variety, preferring to cook coarse ground from scratch for a superior texture. With a naturally sweet taste and a fine gritty texture, fine cornmeal is useful in baking and when used to dust surfaces to stop doughs from sticking. Stoneground is best as it retains more husk, therefore more nutrients, and it is worth noting that cornmeal and polenta as packaged are the same ingredient.

Super Green Polenta + Fritters

Super-green because I've added blitzed cavolo nero to the cooked polenta. Velvety and deep, the polenta makes a brilliant accompaniment to roast lamb or chicken or a tangle of roasted bell peppers. If you would rather serve it as fritters, spread the finished cooked polenta flat on a well-oiled baking tray and leave to cool. Slice to size and reposition on the well-oiled baking tray. Dot with butter or a good slug of olive oil, and grill or bake until hot and crisp in places. Serve immediately, removing the fritters with a fish slice or spatula.

Bring a medium pot of water to the boil with the garlic cloves and the fennel seeds. Add enough salt so that the water tastes fairly salty and add the cavolo nero, pushing it under the water. Cook uncovered until the leaves are tender, about 4–5 minutes.

Drain the cavolo nero well in a colander along with the garlic, then blend to a purée with a pinch of salt to taste and put to one side.

Bring the stock or water to the boil over a high heat. Gradually add the cornmeal/polenta, whisking as you pour. Keep whisking until the polenta starts to thicken and bubbles vigorously.

Turn the heat to low (the polenta should now have just a gentle blip-blip and not be bubbling) and continue to cook, stirring every now and again, until the polenta is tender and forms a thick cohesive mass. This should take about 45 minutes.

Stir in the olive oil or butter, the cavolo nero purée and most of the Parmesan and cook for 1 minute more. Check the seasoning.

Remove from the heat and serve immediately with the remaining Parmesan and plenty of freshly milled black pepper.

5 cloves of garlic, peeled

1 teaspoon fennel seeds

salt and freshly ground black pepper

14oz cavolo nero, thick stems removed (or use curly kale, stems removed)

2¾ pints/6½ cups chicken stock or water

9oz/about 2 cups coarse ground cornmeal/polenta

3½fl oz/just under ½ cup extra virgin olive oil or equivalent in butter

3½oz/1⅓ cups freshly grated Parmesan cheese

7oz/1⅔ cups cornmeal/polenta

4½oz/1 cup self-rising flour

1 medium onion, finely diced

1 x 2oz can of anchovies, drained of oil and finely diced

1 x 14oz can of creamed corn or 1 corn cob, cooked and kernels blended

1 sprig of fresh rosemary, leaves finely chopped

a big pinch–½ teaspoon of red pepper flakes, or to taste

2 large eggs, lightly beaten

salt and freshly ground black pepper

vegetable oil, for frying

lemon wedges, to serve

MAKES ABOUT 8 GOLFBALL-SIZED HUSH PUPPIES

Hush Puppies

Iconic southern American deep-fried nuggets made with cornmeal. Quite apart from having a brilliant name, these hush puppies make the very best sort of snack to serve with a very cold beer. I've upped the ante here by adding creamed corn, anchovies and herbs; experiment and use the batter as a vehicle for flavor.

Heat enough oil for frying in a large frying pan to 350°F—about 1 inch deep should be sufficient.

In a bowl mix the cornmeal/polenta, flour, onion, anchovies, corn, rosemary, red pepper flakes and eggs until blended. Allow to stand for 5 minutes, then add a big pinch of salt and pepper.

Test your oil is hot enough by dropping in a little batter. If it browns and rises immediately, it's ready. Very carefully drop spoonfuls of the mixture into the oil and fry until golden brown.

Don't overcrowd the pan, and leave room for the hush puppies to be turned. Cook them for about 3 minutes, or until golden brown and cooked through. Remove from the oil with a slotted spoon and drain on kitchen paper.

Keep the cooked hush puppies warm in a low oven while cooking the remaining batter. Lightly sprinkle with a bit more salt and pepper to taste, and transfer them to a serving dish.

Serve with lemon wedges.

Carrot Cake

Rice flour is terrific in baking for lending a fine crumb, and is especially good in dense, moist cakes such as this carrot cake.

Preheat the oven to 325°F/gas mark 3 and line an 8-inch cake tin with baking parchment.

In a medium bowl, mix together the ground almonds, rice flour, baking soda, salt and spices and set aside.

In a blender mix together the eggs, oil and sugar.

Add the wet mix to the dry mix and mix just until combined, then gently fold in the raisins and grated carrots.

Pour the batter into the tin and bake for 45 minutes, or until a toothpick inserted in the middle comes out clean.

4½oz/1¼ cups ground almonds

2¾oz/about ½ cup rice flour

1 teaspoon baking soda

a pinch of salt

1½ teaspoons ground cinnamon

½ teaspoon ground ginger

¼ teaspoon freshly grated nutmeg

2 large eggs, at room temperature

2¼fl oz/⅓ cup vegetable oil

2¾oz/⅓ cup light brown sugar

2¾oz/½ cup raisins

5½oz/just over 1 cup finely grated carrots

MAKES 1 X 8-INCH CAKE

2¾oz/¼ cup unsalted butter, melted, plus a little butter or oil for greasing the tin

4 medium-sized very ripe and brown freckled bananas, mashed on a plate with a fork

1 medium egg, beaten

2¾oz/½ cup superfine sugar

1 tablespoon malt extract

1 teaspoon baking soda

a pinch of salt

6½oz/1½ cups rye flour

MAKES A 1LB LOAF

Malted Banana and Rye Bread

Malt extract is a terrific ingredient to use in baking, bread-making and any recipes that call for sugar or honey. An unrefined syrup made from sprouted barley, it is dark brown, thick and very sticky, with a distinctive malty flavor. It is about half as sweet as refined white sugar. It has a good shelf life and you will find yourself using it more and more. For this recipe you can omit the sugar entirely, upping the malt extract or keeping it as is. With the nutty flavor of the rye, the malt works brilliantly here as a trio with the ripe bananas.

Preheat the oven to 325°F/gas mark 3.

Grease a 4-x 8-inch loaf tin with butter or oil.

In a big bowl and using a wooden spoon, mix the melted butter, mashed banana, beaten egg, sugar and malt extract together.

Sprinkle the baking soda and salt over the mixture and mix thoroughly.

Add the rye flour last and mix to combine.

Pour the mixture into the prepared loaf tin.

Bake for 45–50 minutes, or until a skewer inserted into the middle comes out clean.

Cool on a wire rack for 10 minutes before removing from the tin.

Cornbread with Honey, Brown Butter and Oregano

Another American staple and one to rival the hunk of bread made with wheat and served on the side to swipe around the plate, mopping up sauce in lieu of a knife and fork. Cornbread can't really be called healthy, especially if you are like-minded here with the butter in this recipe. Honey and oregano would have some cornbread purists pass out with the shock, but I like it, especially with all that caramelized butter.

7oz/1⅔ cups coarse cornmeal/polenta

9fl oz/1 cup buttermilk

¼ teaspoon baking soda

1 teaspoon baking powder

1 tablespoon runny honey

2 eggs, beaten

1 tablespoon dried oregano

1 teaspoon salt and ½–1 teaspoon freshly ground black pepper

1¾oz/¼ cup butter

1 tablespoon cooking oil

Preheat the oven to 425°F/gas mark 7.

In the hot oven in a baking dish, or on the hob in a dry frying pan over a moderate heat, toast the cornmeal for a few minutes until fragrant.

In a bowl mix the cornmeal with the buttermilk, baking soda, baking powder, honey, eggs, oregano, salt and black pepper to taste.

Put the butter into an 8-inch, non-stick ovenproof frying pan/skillet over a high heat. You want the butter to caramelize, turning nutty, but not burn. Sediments should begin to fall away from the clear hot butter liquid and be a nice shade of brown, not black. Tip all but 2 tablespoons of the caramelized butter into the cornmeal mixture and mix.

Return the pan to a high heat, wait 10 or so seconds for the pan to get very hot, then add the cooking oil and pour in the batter—it should sizzle as it hits the hot pan.

Put the pan into the hot oven and bake for 20–25 minutes, until the cornbread is firm to touch and golden brown or until a skewer inserted into the middle comes out clean.

Remove from the oven and spoon over the reserved brown butter.

Best served immediately, cut into doorstop wedges.

5 SPICE

I keep my spices in an assortment of jam jars with masking tape labels etched boldly in black; their names stretching right around their middles. Some are familiar, household stalwarts, and some sound so exotic that their hastily scrawled name-tapes will stop me in my tracks; they make me want to revisit their smell and then I have to unscrew the jar and take a long, indulgent snort. Sometimes this moment will backfire and the potent contents (now up my nose) will catch me off guard and send me ricocheting around the kitchen in a fit of sneezes. Slipped in among these jars are tiny packets or slivers of tin foil wrapped tight with various powders, pods or seeds brought home from holidays. Their use is sometimes determined not by knowing their name but by where in the world they might have come from.

Not so much a spice rack, my collection of spices spills over a whole shelf, encroaching on the shelves above and below. Stacked up, two or three high, these jars are ever ready to topple. I need more spice shelves, but that would require a bigger kitchen. I could put all these jars out of sight, away in a cupboard, all forlorn. There they might sit, forgotten, their long ago use-by dates an indication of neglect. So, I can't do this either. Instead, with pride of place, from near and far, my spice collection is one that prompts adventure, spurring diversity in my daily cooking, and always encouraging me to use here, there and often. With spices, you will never get bored with the food you cook.

Spices conjure up a different interaction with food and cooking from many other ingredients in the kitchen. In the search for perfume and nuance, spices encourage the cook to dig deep and to smell as much as taste. It's a wonderful feeling to inhale an ingredient and to be transported to another place entirely. Not many ingredients can do this. Sniffing a cauliflower might give you a vegetal jolt of the fields in which it grew, a hunk of beef a whiff of the animal it once was, but chances are the smell will take you thousands of miles away from where you stand. Cinnamon quills might take you to the white sandy beaches of Zanzibar. Turmeric growing wild in the forests of south and south-east Asia. The sun-shrivelled jalapeño fields of Mexico.

In this chapter, I'd like to give you a spice shopping list. There are many spices not included in this, my hit list, and by all means buy others, but these are the spices I think necessary to the pantry and subject to the most thorough use. Buy spices little and often, keeping them vibrant and fresh for cooking with. From these stock spices, I've offered some spice combinations to assemble as and when needed, giving you some heady blends to experiment with.

Key to cooking with spice (and crucially, I'm including black pepper here, salt too for that matter) is to be deliberate when you use it. Aristotle knew a thing or two, and 'the whole is greater than the sum of its parts' is especially pertinent. Spices, like building blocks, give structure. They can help to balance a dish. A brilliant dish that includes spice is made great by the addition of spices from the beginning through to the end. Salt is used from the off to ease out flavor (with the exception of cooking pulses); an assertive grind of black pepper at the table gives a hypnotizing heat; using whole dried chili or cinnamon quills to swell and permeate a dish as it cooks, or the crackle of cumin seeds in a tarka before any other ingredients are added, imbues the dish with smokiness and depth. Be confident. A dish should taste of the spices you use. Give spices their full workout—toast and grind them fresh for use where indicated. And lastly, my pinches are almost always generous and never really all that parsimonious.

PANTRY BASICS

sea salt

black pepper

whole allspice

cardamom pods

red pepper flakes

cinnamon sticks/quills

ground cinnamon

cloves

coriander seeds

cumin seeds

fennel seeds

ground ginger

whole nutmeg

paprika, hot (picante), sweet (dulce) and smoked

saffron strands

Sichuan pepper

star anise

sumac

ground turmeric

vanilla pods

curry powder

five-spice powder

garam masala

herbes de Provence

ras el hanout

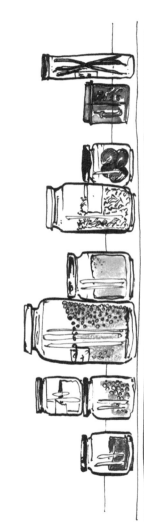

Key Individual Spices

Buy little and often from supermarkets, grocery stores or online. Choose shops with a high turnover of spices—freshness is key. Toast whole spices in a dry frying pan until fragrant, and add whole or grind fresh for use. On my shelves in small amounts and replenished often are:

ALLSPICE
Buy the whole berries, toast and grind finely or use whole, remembering to watch out for them in the finished dish.

BLACK PEPPER
Always grind from fresh, coarse or fine, to your liking.

CARDAMOM
Buy whole pods, crush, remove the husk and grind the seeds or use whole, crushed, remembering to watch out for them in the finished dish. Black cardamom is worth seeking out for an intriguing and smoky cardamom flavor.

RED PEPPER FLAKES
Red pepper flakes (find a variety you prefer to use; I like Turkish red and black red pepper flakes for a sweet hot or smoky heat).

CINNAMON
Use whole quills and also buy ground cinnamon. Pop whole quills in dishes as they cook to permeate, and use ground in cakes and such.

CLOVES
Buy whole to toast and grind or use whole, remembering to watch out for them in the finished dish.

CORIANDER SEEDS
Whole seeds; toast and grind roughly or finely as you like or leave whole.

CUMIN SEEDS
Whole seeds; toast and grind roughly or finely as you like or leave whole.

FENNEL SEEDS
Toast, roughly crack, grind finely or leave whole.

GINGER
Buy ground ginger little and often (fresh ginger is also a refrigerator staple).

NUTMEG

Have whole nutmeg to grate as needed.

PAPRIKA

Hot (picante), bittersweet and hot (agridulce) and sweet and mild (dulce) paprika are all wonderful and used to your taste; smoked (pimentón de La Vera) is a different seasoning and should be used more sensitively.

SAFFRON

Buy saffron strands to soak in a splash of warm water for 15 minutes and give them a gentle bash to release yet more color and flavor. Use the saffron and the water.

SICHUAN PEPPER

Despite its name, not a pepper but the seeds of the prickly ash. Worth sourcing some for its unique citrus flavor with a numbing tingly buzzing sensation. One of the five ingredients in 5-spice powder. Use whole or grind to a powder.

STAR ANISE

Use whole mostly to permeate in cooking, or you can grind for use.

SUMAC

Ground red-purple berries. Sour and aromatic, use as you might lemon for a tart fruity burst of flavor. Look for freshly ground sumac; the good stuff should leave an oily moist residue on your fingers as you take a pinch.

TURMERIC

Buy ground turmeric powder, little and often. Fresh is sometimes available, but the powder is far more common.

VANILLA

Buy pods to split, and scrape out the seeds and sticky bits for use. Keep the scraped pods in jars of superfine sugar for vanilla-scented sugar.

Ready-made Spice Blends

No shame in buying these powerhouse blends ready-made and off the shelf—they are an easy shortcut to flavor. Find a brand you like and buy little and often. Do buy blends with a recent production date and a long sell-by date. Refresh frequently, keeping the blends tip-top.

CURRY POWDER, HOT OR MILD

Curry powder usually contains a mixture of turmeric, chili powder, ground cumin, coriander, black pepper and ginger, all fine spices in their own right, mixed here for a general seasoning. Use as a base note and add extra spices as you wish.

FIVE-SPICE (CHINESE)

A terrific blend sometimes confused with allspice (a berry from the Pimenta dioica tree). Five-spice is a spurious name, given there are no typical five spices that make up the blend. Star anise and cinnamon will always feature, and often Sichuan pepper and others such as ginger, fennel, cloves and nutmeg. Use in Chinese and Vietnamese dishes.

GARAM MASALA

There are many south Asian regional variations of masala. Garam masala is a northern Indian/Pakistani blend. Blend any combination of spices for your own unique masala, but a good garam is a great starting point.

HERBES DE PROVENCE

An easy seasoning blend to flavor your food with a blast of the Mediterranean. Dried herbs are very different from fresh but I love their earthy pungency at times. Usual suspects in a good herbes de Provence might include any one of this heady selection of sun-soaked herbs: rosemary, savory, thyme, marjoram, sometimes lavender and fennel seeds. Lemon zest is fairly typical too.

RAS EL HANOUT

From North Africa, 'ras el hanout' translates loosely as 'head of the shop', meaning the best spices on offer at any given time. Much like the garams of India, there is no definitive configuration for ras el hanout, and the combination can very much be down to the person making the blend. More than twelve and up to twenty different spices can be a common scenario, including cardamom, cumin, clove, cinnamon, nutmeg, mace, allspice, ground ginger, chili peppers, coriander seeds, various peppercorns including long or cubeb, sweet or hot paprika, fenugreek, ground turmeric, dried rose petals, grains of paradise, fennel seeds, aniseed and galangal.

SPICE COMBINATIONS

Mix up these blends little and often—any surplus will spur you to use it up in your cooking, adding flair and flavor. Store in a screwtop jar to add to recipes when you want to season any dishes of specific origin, when one or two spices just won't do.

Italian Fennel Seed

I use a lot of fennel seeds in my kitchen—in conjunction with garlic, chili and fresh or dried herbs, fennel seeds give gorgeous warm floral aniseed notes to much of my Italian cooking.

2 parts dried oregano/marjoram/thyme (or you can use fresh rosemary or sage)

1 part crushed fennel seeds

½ part red pepper flakes (optional)

½ part cracked black pepper

Quatre Épices

A classic French spice blend popular in charcuterie and one-pot slow-cooked stews and casseroles. Allspice is the key note here, with nutmeg, ginger and cloves bringing up the rear. Some recipes list pepper instead of allspice, but I think this is a mistake. Allspice is one of my very favourite spices, a gorgeous combination of cinnamon, nutmeg and clove in profile. Use in Caramelised apple and maple bread pudding on page 290.

6 parts ground allspice (replace with ground pepper for purely savoury version)

2½ parts freshly grated nutmeg

2 parts ground ginger (or use cinnamon if you prefer)

½ parts ground cloves

Baharat

The name 'baharat' means 'spice' in Arabic. It is an indispensable seasoning to add to any Middle Eastern-inspired cooking. Crucially the blend will always include black pepper and allspice with cinnamon. Other spices can be added to the blend according to preference. Saffron, clove, nutmeg, paprika, ginger, cardamom, turmeric and chili powder are all a good match. A Turkish-style baharat might include dried mint (nane) or dried oregano (kekik), whereas in North Africa, dried rose petals might be ground and added to the blend. Add baharat to pilaf, tomato sauces, to freshly popped corn for a spicy snack, or use the blend as a rub to season meat or fish before cooking. Add neutral oil to some baharat to use as a marinade, or mix with olive oil to serve as a condiment for dipping raw vegetables or grilled flatbreads into.

BAHARAT 1 (MORE FLORAL)
2 parts ground allspice

3 parts ground cinnamon

1 part freshly grated nutmeg

1 part ground cloves

1 part ground coriander

2 parts freshly ground black pepper

1 part ground ginger

BAHARAT 2 (MORE PUNCHY)
3 parts freshly ground black pepper

3 parts paprika (unsmoked)

3 parts ground cumin

2 parts ground cinnamon

2 parts ground coriander

1 part freshly grated nutmeg

1 part ground cloves

1 part ground cardamom

Dukkah

A Middle Eastern ground spice mix that includes hazelnuts. Often served with olive oil as a condiment to serve with bread to dip as an appetizer, Or add to salads, pilafs or soups, or sprinkle on roasted vegetables, or use it as a seasoning crust to grill meat or fish. Use as is or coarsely ground.

4 parts toasted white sesame seeds

2 parts toasted coriander seeds

2 parts toasted, peeled and finely chopped hazelnuts

1½ parts toasted ground cumin

½ part cracked black pepper

½ part salt

Salt and Pepper Mix

Boost everyday salt and pepper seasoning with Sichuan pepper (a numbing, tingling berry) and red pepper flakes. Make this in small quantities and use as you would salt and pepper.

½ part black peppercorns, toasted and coarsely ground

½ part Sichuan peppercorns, toasted and coarsely ground

¼–½ part red pepper flakes

1 part flaky salt

2¼oz/¼ cup salt

10½oz/2¼ cups whole almonds, unskinned

2 tablespoons groundnut oil, or use olive oil

1-2 tablespoons spice blend options (see pages 162–4), or to taste

MAKES 10½OZ/2¼ CUPS

Brined and Roasted Spiced Almonds

Salt falls off roasted almonds. So brine them instead! Use any nut and experiment with spice blends. Ras el hanout or garam masala and either of the baharats on page 164 are a favourite.

Bring the salt and 7fl oz/¾ cup of water to the boil in a medium saucepan (just to dissolve the salt). Then allow to cool for 5 minutes.

Add the almonds and soak for 30 minutes.

Preheat the oven to 375°F/gas mark 5.

Drain the almonds, patting them dry with kitchen paper or a clean dish towel. Spread them on a baking tray or in an ovenproof dish and add the oil and your preferred spice blend, to taste. Use your hands and mix well to coat.

Roast the almonds in the oven, shaking the tray often, until toasted through and fragrant, 20–30 minutes. Remove from the oven and cool before storing in a tin.

Chili Oil

There is such a thing as a bad chili oil and that's one that has sat around for too long, grown stale and lost its luster. Make your own chili oil and use it liberally in any recipes that call for oil and also chili. Use a neutral vegetable or sunflower oil, never olive oil. This version is particularly delicious, with tingly Sichuan pepper, sesame and star anise, among others.

10fl oz/1¼ cups vegetable oil
1 tablespoon Sichuan peppercorns
2 star anise
½ a cinnamon stick
2 bay leaves
4 tablespoons red pepper flakes, or more to taste
1 tablespoon sesame seeds
½ teaspoon salt

MAKES ABOUT 10FL OZ

Heat the oil, Sichuan peppercorns, star anise, cinnamon and bay leaves in a small saucepan over a medium-high heat and simmer for 2 minutes.

Add the red pepper flakes, sesame seeds and salt, stir well and leave to cool to room temperature. Transfer the oil along with the chili and sesame sediments to a glass jar and seal.

Homemade Chili Sauce

Remove the seeds from the chili as you prepare this sauce if you want to reduce the heat. Equally, for a green chili sauce, you can use green chilies and bell peppers.

Blend all the ingredients until smooth.

In a saucepan over a high heat, bring the sauce to the boil. Reduce to a simmer and cook for 10–15 minutes, until you have the thickness you'd like. Taste and adjust, balancing the flavor with additional vinegar, sugar or some salt where necessary.

Take off the heat and cool.

Transfer the chili sauce to a clean jar or bottle. Stored in the refrigerator, it will keep for up to 2 weeks.

2 tablespoons vegetable oil

9oz/2 cups fresh red chilies, roughly sliced

7oz/1½ cups red peppers, roughly chopped

7 cloves of garlic, peeled and left whole

2½fl oz/⅓ cup cider, white wine or white rice vinegar

2 tablespoons tomato paste, or use ½ x 14oz can of tomatoes (about 7oz/1 cup)

4 tablespoons light brown or caster sugar

1–3 tablespoons fish sauce (according to your taste)

MAKES ABOUT 18FL OZ

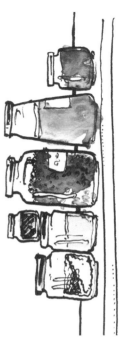

Masala Chai

Easy to make and so much better than any shop-bought chai. Find the combination of spices that you like best. Best drunk sweet, very early in the morning and just as you're about to board a train.

Put the quantity of spices you are using into a saucepan, and add 9fl oz/1 cup of cold water per serving.

Bring to the boil over a high heat, then reduce the heat, partially cover the pan and simmer gently for 5 minutes.

Remove from the heat and add 1 teabag per serving, then leave to steep for about 4 minutes.

Strain out the spices and tea bags or leaves , and add milk and sugar to taste. Gently heat the chai, stirring until the sugar dissolves.

Serve immediately.

black tea, bags or leaves, milk and sugar

MAIN SPICES
green cardamom (crack the pods)

fresh ginger, or use ground

cinnamon stick, or use ground

SECONDARY SPICES
fennel seeds, toasted and lightly bashed

nutmeg, freshly grated

black peppercorns, freshly ground or just cracked

coriander seeds, toasted and cracked

whole cloves (caution here, as too many will make your chai too musky and strong)

FOR EXAMPLE, ONE CUP OF CHAI COULD INCLUDE THE FOLLOWING:
2 cardamom pods, cracked

3 whole black peppercorns, freshly ground or cracked

¼ teaspoon fennel seeds, toasted and lightly bashed

½ a cinnamon stick, or ground cinnamon to taste

2–3 slices of fresh ginger, or ground ginger to taste

Spiced Hot Chocolate

Proper hot chocolate, made by melting grated chocolate in hot milk, is incredible. Adding spice is no news flash—just think of your favorite speciality chocolate bar and ape those flavors. Chili, cinnamon, ginger, cardamom and vanilla are some of my favorite spices combined with chocolate. Use dark chocolate for a richer drink, or milk chocolate if you prefer your hot chocolate to be less intense. Any which way, you want it satin smooth and piping hot. A small pinch of salt will also boost flavor.

Grate the chocolate into a bowl.

Warm the milk with the spice(s) to boiling point and add the salt.

Pour the hot milk over the grated chocolate and whisk to combine.

Serve immediately.

FOR 2

2¾–3½oz chocolate, dark or milk, as you like

18fl oz/2 cups milk

spice(s) of choice (see recipe introduction)

a small pinch of salt

6 REFRIGERATOR AND FREEZER

I don't have a large refrigerator and sometimes when other people open my refrigerator they remark upon how empty it is. 'A chef's refrigerator,' I say, and they often look puzzled. Wouldn't a chef's refrigerator be stuffed full of ingredients to cook with? It sometimes is, at Christmas or on other occasions when I expect to feed a crowd, but as anyone who is interested in cooking will know, cooking on a daily basis means maintaining a steady turnover of food and ingredients. The movement of food from uncooked to cooked gives a sense of rhythm to the comings and goings of the refrigerator. Raw ingredients become finished dishes, then return to the refrigerator or freezer as all-important leftovers. A holding pen for ingredients, the contents of my refrigerator say an awful lot about how I shop and cook, week in week out.

The exception to this fast turnover of ingredients in my refrigerator is the top shelf, home to an international selection of preserves, pickles and condiments. These are all pungent ingredients, used more sparingly and with a longer shelf life; various jars, bottles and tubs, shop-bought, homemade, some labeled and some not. Their worth in the kitchen is that they all pack a punch as spoonfuls and handfuls or served as accompaniments. There is often mustard (Dijon and grain), miso, tamarind pulp, Korean red pepper paste (gojuchang), Chinese fermented black beans, jars of capers, anchovies and olives and usually a big jar of shop-bought Polish sour pickled cucumbers, all cloudy with dill. With the pickles long gone, I never throw away the juice but use it to dress chop chop salads (see page 55), in bread doughs in lieu of some of the water for an impossible-to-identify, intriguing sourness, or as a general piquant seasoning liquid, for example in cabbage and caraway soup (see page 228). Kimchi, Korean fermented vegetables, is for me an essential grocery item. Eaten refrigerator-cold, sour, crunchy and hot, kimchi with steamed rice and broccoli is one of my laziest suppers and the one I relish the most for its simplicity. There might also be some rhubarb ketchup I've made myself, an assortment of Indian pickles in jars, or some blueberries pickled to accompany the ham one Christmas back. On the rare occasions (time, inclination and curiosity) that I delve to the back of the refrigerator, it is there that I will come across something more esoteric, like the jar of bergamots in syrup bought in Italy or the plastic tub of sausage casings all frosted with rock salt.

In the door of the refrigerator there is always milk. I have three young children, so I buy full fat. There never seems to be enough, milk-guzzlers all three, and we forever run out. On the shelf above the milk sits butter. Butter is tremendous to eat and to cook with. I never buy so-called spread, finding it oleaginous in name and substance. I've worked in restaurants where butter use has been so flagrant, the butter had to have its own refrigerator. Yogurt features often in the food I make at home and I am never without a large tub of plain yogurt in the refrigerator to use as a marinade, in lassi, on porridge or bircher, in cakes or stabilized with flour and egg and cooked with rice for yogurt and rice soup (see page 186). This recipe stands out here as one of my favorite recipes in the book. Crème fraîche or sour cream, though less frequently used than yogurt, has an equally good shelf life and will always find a use.

As for cheese, all the best people I have known in food and kitchens share a deep and greedy love of it. In London once I worked in a cheese shop—a brief break from cooking at the stoves. I wanted to learn more about cheese. And I did. I learned about the different milks used to make certain cheeses, from Alpine cow's to Staffordshire goat's and Italian sheep's.

How some cheeses are washed and some are cave aged. How proper blue cheeses should never have crude and uniform injection marks from the mold but should be marbled sensitively throughout with a deep and beautiful blue. Hard cheeses with salty crunchy crystals, mountain cheeses made in monasteries, and soft voluptuous cheeses barely able to hold their form; bursting at the rind . . . I still often think about those cheeses. Good cheese should always be a treat. In my refrigerator and used more frequently are any one of a good-quality Cheddar, halloumi, ricotta, mozzarella or feta. Knockout individual cheeses are certain to arrive and depart readily from the refrigerator on special occasions.

Eggs should be stored at a constant temperature below 68°F, which in most domestic kitchens means the refrigerator. This avoids temperature fluctuations, which can alter the porosity of the shell. Egg storage is a contentious issue, with a split between those who keep their eggs in the refrigerator and those who don't. I keep my eggs in the refrigerator. My kitchen is small and can get quite hot in the summer or if the oven is on, and the refrigerator is a reliably cool storage place for eggs and helps to maintain their quality. I also store my eggs in their original cardboard carton and never in the fabricated plastic egg box in the door of the refrigerator. The cardboard cartons help to reduce moisture loss and protect the eggs from absorbing other refrigerator flavors. The opening and closing of the door can also be disruptive to the egg's form and temperature. As for cold eggs having a reputation for being trickier to bake with, I am in the habit of removing eggs destined for baking an hour or so before use to acclimatize. Eggs are a miracle food, and there is nothing I can write that hasn't already been written. Without eggs, my cooking comes to a grinding halt; they are the breakfast lunch and dinner to my life.

Next to the eggs in a wide tub with a lid sit some brined pickled vegetables. Quick pickled, these vegetables won't last indefinitely like brined and long-fermented pickles. Prepare the pickles the day before you serve them and use the excess vinegar in salad dressings and marinades. Serve the pickles as antipasti at the start of a meal, or sliced and added to cheese, ham or hard-boiled egg sandwiches, or use them in salads and chopped into mayonnaise like you might with capers or gherkins. The steady depletion of this pickle tub is determined by just how moreish these sweet-sour vegetables are.

Vegetable drawers can be funny things, a bit like vegetable graveyards. In mine there is stock celery and carrots, a cucumber (always a cucumber), some lettuce and lots of apples. Refrigerator-cold apples are the best; they are my guilty secret and I love their cold juicy crunch. The vegetable drawer is not where I look for stimulus to cook but where I rely upon the contents to support the food I cook. Celery and carrots are the fulcrum for my love affair with lentils, which is why I am never without either, but they will rarely feature as a showpiece vegetable come lunch or supper. I love vegetables and relish their seasonal bounty, but they are best eaten soon after purchase. Which is why, in my house, any vegetable hoard will sit royally ready for use slap bang in the center of the kitchen table, much like the fruit bowl. Herbs, however optimistically I refrigerate them, never seem to last all that well. Bay leaves, sage, thyme, rosemary and even leafy robust parsley, these are all hardy enough to survive out of the refrigerator, ready and waiting. Soft herbs— basil, mint, cilantro, dill, chives and tarragon—are far better used flamboyantly and without a care for conservation; they have no place in the refrigerator.

I am, however, conscious of the modern-day reliance on refrigerating absolutely everything, when often there is no need. On a cold winter's day, the doorstep is a fine place for milk to sit. I love that my mum uses the windowsill in her front porch as an extension of the refrigerator when all the family descend at Christmas and her refrigerator is fit to burst. I am proud of the paucity of my refrigerator. Its bare bones represent the fact that I let nothing go to waste and that I always strive to use any ingredients at their optimum quality.

My freezer might raise even more eyebrows than my refrigerator. Packed tight in plastic bags are my favorite dresses and most treasured jumpers. I remember staying with my aunt a few years ago and feeling quite spooked by the fact that her freezer was full of clothes, stashed and frozen in shopping bags. Had she murdered someone and was she hiding the evidence? 'Moths,' she said casually; 'it's only way to save your clothes.' She was right—like Jenny, I now freeze any items I'm terrified the moths will want to munch. They're a hungry bunch and, try as I might, they are a devil to get rid of. Freezing is the only solution, though some garments are a little chilly of a morning!

I enjoy cooking daily, and the thought of cooking something to freeze and eat on another day is anathema to me. As such, I rarely use my freezer to store excess food (it tends to all get eaten) or ready-made meals. Cooking is an incredibly emotive activity: what I want to cook will depend on what mood I am in, who I am feeding or what ingredients I have to hand. I can't imagine having the forethought to cook something for a day yet to happen. There are exceptions I suppose, the arrival of a new baby in the house for example, when all is a bleary bubble—then, absolutely, some frozen previously made meals are a lifesaver. Like the refrigerator, my freezer is kept pretty spartan; squashed in among the clothes are always frozen peas and spinach, fresh curry leaves I've bought by the branch (they freeze brilliantly), filo pastry and endlessly reliable wholemeal pita breads for packed lunches, fattoush salads, with falafel (see page 66), ful medames (see page 64) or baked eggs (see page 90).

Frozen spinach is a relatively new freezer favorite for me. Fresh spinach is wonderful, but bought by the bag from the supermarket the yield is always low and big leafy bunches from greengrocers are often hard to come by. Defrosted and added to any wet soupy dishes such as coconut and egg curry (see page 188) or heated through with cream and mustard, frozen spinach is a useful staple. Like peas, spinach fares particularly well flash-frozen and retains many of its nutrients. Frozen peas are a reliable substitute for fresh, especially any bigger peas, which can be floury in texture, with tough skins. With no real need to cook, thawed and thrown in rice dishes, dhals, curries and salads, or crushed and spiced for samosas-like filo parcels (see page 200), or heated with oil and mint for sott'olio (see page 198), my freezer is never without frozen peas. Widely available, filo pastry is also well suited to the freezer. Defrosted just enough for it to no longer be brittle, in a flash these paper-thin translucent sheets of dough, brushed with melted butter or olive oil, can be formed to make any number of crisp pies or delicate crusts. Use it to make quick samosa-like parcels (see page 200) or pumpkin and feta pie (see page 196), among others.

I see the refrigerator and freezer very much as a continuation of my pantry. Cannily stocked with key staples as suggested, and working in conjunction with the dry store, I am able to produce assorted delicious and economical dishes daily. To finish—as if to close the door on this chapter—I have a friend who swears by the fact that she will sometimes open her refrigerator door and scream something, anything, into the refrigerator as a therapeutic release from the bedlam of parenthood. I know this feeling all too well. When all around you is shambolic and no one is listening to anyone, shouting into this plastic abyss—door wide open and your head in the quiet of the cool—is an entirely liberating and sensible thing to do. Flashpoint over, serendipity is the bottle of wine in the door of the refrigerator.

REFRIGERATOR AND FREEZER BASICS

REFRIGERATOR

milk

butter

plain yogurt

crème fraîche

Cheddar cheese

halloumi

feta

mozzarella

eggs

FREEZER

spinach

petits pois

filo pastry

pita bread

curry leaves

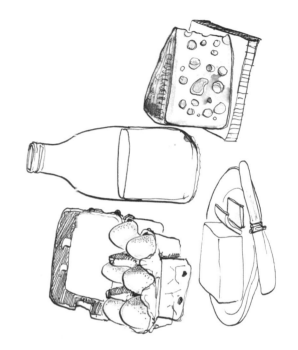

Halloumi Saganaki

Brined cheese, halloumi has a tremendous shelf life and my refrigerator is rarely without it. Saganaki is a Greek preparation using this well-loved squeaky cheese. Dip the slices into beaten egg and roll them in semolina and sesame seeds before frying, then drench with honey and dried oregano. Squeeze over lemon and serve with chopped fresh ripe figs, peaches, apricots or some grapes, with good bread to mop up the juices.

a handful of fine semolina, or use all-purpose flour

1 tablespoon sesame seeds

9oz block of halloumi cheese

1 egg, beaten

3 tablespoons olive oil

2 tablespoons runny honey

lemon, to squeeze, plus lemon wedges, to serve

½ teaspoon dried oregano

a pinch of red pepper flakes (optional)

2 green onions, sliced (optional)

Mix the semolina or flour and sesame seeds together.

Cut the halloumi into thick slices. Dip the slices in the beaten egg, then roll in the flour mix.

Heat the olive oil in a non-stick frying pan and fry the cheese on a medium heat for about 2 minutes on each side, until golden brown.

Drizzle with the honey and a squeeze of lemon and sprinkle with oregano, and red pepper flakes and green onions, if liked. Serve with lemon wedges.

Turkish Eggs with Yogurt, Dill and Brown Butter

This breakfast staple in Turkey, made by poaching the eggs and serving them in seasoned yogurt spooned over with melted brown butter, all spiky with chili and paprika, is sensational. Serve with toasted pita to scoop up the egg and the warm, spicy yogurt. Chopped ripe tomato, avocado or cooked spinach, chard or kale are also welcome.

10½oz/1½ cups Greek yogurt

1 tablespoon finely chopped fresh dill

1 clove of garlic, crushed to a paste

salt and freshly ground black pepper

1¾oz/¼ cup unsalted butter

1 teaspoon red pepper flakes, preferably Turkish Aleppo

½ teaspoon paprika, sweet, not hot or smoked

2fl oz/just under ¼ cup white vinegar

8 eggs

toasted pita bread, to serve

Stir together the yogurt, dill, garlic, and salt and pepper to taste in a bowl. Divide between four warmed serving bowls and keep somewhere warm.

Melt the butter in a small pan until it foams and nut-brown sediments begin to fall away in the liquid butter. Remove from the heat and add the red pepper flakes, a pinch of salt and the paprika. Set aside and keep warm.

Boil a large saucepan of water without salt. Reduce the heat to medium and add the vinegar. Poach the eggs to your liking (a firmish white but with the yolk still runny will be about 3 minutes). Using a slotted spoon, transfer the eggs to kitchen paper to drain.

Divide the poached eggs between the four bowls of yogurt and spoon over the melted spiced butter. Serve immediately, with the toasted pita.

1¾ pints/4 cups chicken stock
or water

5½oz/¾ cup white rice

1 tablespoon all-purpose flour

2 teaspoons dried mint

1lb 2oz/2½ cups Greek yoghurt

salt

1 egg

1oz/2 tablespoons butter

1 tablespoon red pepper flakes,
preferably Turkish (Urfa or Aleppo)

lemon, to squeeze (optional)

Yogurt Soup

Another Turkish preparation here. I've written yogurt soup recipes before, but this version includes rice. This recipe is a tonic for anyone in need of gentle replenishment. Simple, so brilliant.

Bring the stock to the boil in a large saucepan and add the rice. Stir well and simmer for about 20–25 minutes, until the rice is tender and has thickened the liquid. Remove from the heat.

In a bowl mix the flour, half the mint, the yogurt, about ½ teaspoon of salt and the egg.

Pour the yogurt mixture into the rice and mix well, then simmer gently for another 10 minutes, or until the soup has a creamy consistency, stirring to avoid lumps. Check the seasoning.

Heat the butter in a small pan and when it foams add the rest of the dried mint and the red pepper flakes and cook for 30 seconds. Add a squeeze of lemon juice if you like.

Pour the butter over the soup and serve.

Lassi

A good blender is essential. You want the yogurt to blitz with the other ingredients in such a fury that the mix turns pale and frothy. Drink immediately. And then drink more.

Put the yogurt, sugar, rose water, cardamom pods and water into the blender. Process for 1 minute, then add the ice and process for a minute more.

Strain and serve in tall glasses.

1lb 5oz/3 cups plain yogurt

3oz/about ½ cup superfine sugar

1 tablespoon rose water (or to taste)

3 whole cardamom pods (optional)

7fl oz/¾ cup cold water

3½oz/about ½ cup crushed ice cubes

3 tablespoons vegetable oil

2 onions, finely diced

4–6 cloves of garlic, finely sliced or chopped, to taste

1 green chili pepper, finely sliced, or use red pepper flakes to taste (about 1 teaspoon)

½ teaspoon sugar

6 cardamom pods, bashed and husks removed

1 level tablespoon curry powder (hot or mild, as you like)

1 cinnamon stick

1 teaspoon ground turmeric

8 eggs

1lb 2oz/2½ cups thawed frozen spinach,

1 tablespoon fresh tamarind paste or 1 teaspoon tamarind powder

1 x 14fl oz can of coconut milk

about 1 teaspoon of each salt and freshly ground black pepper

rice and pickles, to serve

Egg, Turmeric and Coconut Curry

This gently spiced curry, fragrant with coconut milk and spice, is incredibly quick to make and showcases the humble frozen spinach to spectacular effect. Cook as many eggs as you would like to serve. Serve with brown or white rice and jarred Indian pickles.

Heat the oil in a large saucepan over a moderate heat, then add the onions and cook until soft and translucent, 8–10 minutes. Add the garlic, chili, sugar and all the spices apart from the tamarind and fry for a further 2–3 minutes.

Meanwhile, put the eggs into a saucepan and cover with cold water. Put a lid on the pan and bring to the boil. As soon as the water begins to boil, time the eggs for 6 minutes. Remove from the heat and set aside until comfortably cool enough to peel and halve.

Add the thawed spinach, tamarind and the coconut milk to the spiced onion mix and heat through. Add the eggs and season with salt and pepper.

Serve immediately, with rice and Indian pickles.

Whipped Feta

7oz feta cheese

7oz/¾ cup Greek yoghurt

juice of ½ a lemon

2 tablespoons extra virgin olive oil

1 teaspoon sumac

Again, a cheese with longevity—stock some in your refrigerator to serve as a cheese, or whip into a dip, or use it to bake with. Many recipes for whipped feta recommend using a food processor to break down the cheese, but I don't bother. I find it is just as quick to use a bowl and whisk to whip the cheese, mellowing it with the yogurt. Serve as a dip with toasted pita and raw vegetables. I've doused the mix here with olive oil, and sumac; toasted seeds, red pepper flakes and chopped herbs are all equally good.

Put the feta and yogurt into a mixing bowl and whisk until the feta is completely broken up and becomes creamy.

Add the lemon juice and mix again.

Put the dip into a serving bowl and dress the surface with the olive oil and sumac.

Crème Fraîche-marinated Mozzarella

Mozzarella is at its best when eaten young. Good-quality mozzarella can be expensive, and this recipe extends the portion size with the addition of crème fraîche. Spooned over the slices of mozzarella, the crème fraîche begins to ever so slightly coagulate, making the ingredients more than the sum of their own parts. Serve as a light lunch or a first course, with some garlic-rubbed toast and a green salad or grilled summer vegetables.

Whisk the crème fraîche with 1 tablespoon of olive oil, the garlic and lemon juice, and season with salt and pepper.

Arrange the mozzarella on a large dish—slightly overlapping is fine—then drizzle over about 2 tablespoons of olive oil. Spoon the seasoned crème fraîche over the mozzarella.

Sprinkle the lemon zest and red pepper flakes halves evenly over the plate.

Set to one side for the flavors to meld and for the mozzarella and the crème fraîche to knit slightly, at least 1 hour and up to 3.

To serve, add the herbs and a final tablespoon of olive oil.

7oz/1 cup crème fraîche

approx. 4 tablespoons olive oil

½ clove of garlic, crushed

grated zest of 1 lemon and juice of ½ a lemon

salt and freshly ground black pepper

2 balls of buffalo mozzarella, sliced into thick disks, about 5 per ball

½–1 teaspoon red pepper flakes (to taste)

a small bunch of fresh marjoram, oregano, basil or mint, leaves roughly chopped

9oz/about 2 cups diced Swiss
cheese, such as Gruyère, at room
temperature

1 egg yolk

1 tablespoon Worcestershire sauce

1 teaspoon Dijon mustard

a pinch of cayenne pepper, or use
red pepper flakes

2 or 3 tablespoons cream, to thin
the cheese mixture if needed

salt

12 slices of good white bread,
crusts removed

12 thin slices of prosciutto, or
another cured ham

olive oil, for frying

SERVES 6

Harry's Bar Sandwich

**Harry's Bar in Venice is a landmark restaurant and
inventor of the classic peach Bellini, beef carpaccio
and this sandwich, arguably one of the very best
fried cheese sandwiches ever created. Mustard,
Worcestershire sauce and cayenne pepper all give
pep to the melted cheese. Unfried, the prepared
sandwiches can keep for a day or two if wrapped
and kept in the refridgerator**

Put the diced cheese, egg yolk, Worcestershire sauce,
mustard and cayenne in a food processor and process
until smooth, thinning with a bit of cream if it is too
thick to spread.

Add salt to taste, then check the seasoning, adding more
of any of the flavorings to suit your taste.

Spread the cheese mixture over one side of each bread
slice. Lay the ham over 6 of the slices, and top with the
remaining 6 slices of bread, cheese-side down. Press the
sandwiches together firmly.

Heat a frying pan over a medium-high heat until quite
hot and add a thin film of oil.

Add as many sandwiches as will fit the pan and fry,
turning once, until they are golden brown and crisp.
Repeat with the remaining sandwiches, adding more
oil to the pan as necessary.

Drain on kitchen paper, then cut into pieces and
serve straight away, wrapped in a paper napkin or
baking parchment.

Baked Feta and Sourdough with Olives and Oregano

Baked feta is wonderful. The heat of the oven works a treat on this salty cheese, blistering the cubes on the outside and turning the insides melted and soft. With toasted bread, collapsed sweet roasted tomatoes and olives, this is a dish to share at the table, with a salad of lettuce and cucumber dressed with lemon, salt and olive oil, for example.

Preheat the oven to 350°F/gas mark 4.

Combine the feta, tomatoes, olives, sourdough and oil in an ovenproof dish and add the black pepper, oregano and red pepper flakes.

Cook in the oven for about 30 minutes, or until the tomatoes are completely soft and the feta and bread are beginning to turn golden.

9oz feta cheese, cut into approx. 8 pieces

7oz (about 15) cherry tomatoes, halved

15 or so Kalamata olives, pitted and roughly chopped

7oz sourdough bread, day-old, crusts off and torn into chunks the same size as the feta

2 tablespoons olive oil

approx. 1 teaspoon freshly ground black pepper,

1 tablespoon dried oregano

½–1 teaspoon red pepper flakes, to taste

SERVES 4 AS A LIGHT LUNCH

Aligot

A regional French dish from the Massif Central. Whipping the potatoes with the cheese, cream, garlic, salt and pepper until smooth and slightly elastic makes it astonishingly good. It's traditionally made with a Tomme cheese, but a good Cheddar will work here. Serve just warm, with some fried fat French style sausages (Toulouse), cornichons or gherkins, boiled new potatoes and some crusty bread. It's a Sunday night treat sort of supper.

Boil the potatoes in salted water until tender. Drain, then either mash or put them through a potato ricer. Return the potatoes to the pan you used to boil them and put them over a very low heat to keep warm.

Stir in the butter, garlic and cream. Gradually add the cheese a handful at a time, beating with a wooden spoon as you go.

Once you have incorporated all the cheese, add salt and pepper to taste and serve immediately.

1lb 5oz floury potatoes (about a dozen medium-sized)

salt and freshly ground black pepper

1¾oz/¼ cup butter

1–2 cloves of garlic, finely minced or crushed, to taste

2 tablespoons crème fraîche, sour or heavy cream

14oz/4 cups grated Cheddar cheese,

12oz pumpkin or butternut squash, peeled and cut into ¾ inch dice

2¾oz/⅔ cup pine nuts or chopped walnuts

1 onion, finely diced

1 tablespoon olive oil

7oz/1½ cups crumbled feta cheese

3½oz/½ cup cottage cheese, ricotta or quark

2 eggs, beaten

3 teaspoons dried oregano

¼ teaspoon ground cinnamon

¼ teaspoon freshly grated nutmeg

approx. 1 teaspoon each of salt and freshly ground black pepper

10½oz filo pastry sheets

3½oz/½ cup melted butter

1 teaspoon nigella seeds (or use sesame)

1 tablespoon runny honey

1 teaspoon red pepper flakes

Spiced Filo Pumpkin Pie

Blisteringly crisp filo pastry stuffed full with spiced pumpkin and curd. Hot out of the oven, drench with honey, red pepper and oregano for an impressive lunch, or take it to eat cold on a picnic.

Preheat the oven to 400°F/gas mark 6. Put the pumpkin or squash on a baking tray and roast for about 30 minutes, until tender. Put the pine nuts or walnuts on a separate tray and put into the oven for the last 5 minutes.

Meanwhile, fry the onion in the olive oil for about 8–10 minutes, until soft and translucent.

Lower the oven temperature to 375°F/gas mark 5. Line a baking sheet with baking parchment and set aside.

In a bowl mix the cooked pumpkin, pine nuts, cooked onion, feta, cottage cheese, beaten eggs, 2 teaspoons of oregano, the cinnamon, nutmeg and salt and pepper.

Put the prepared baking sheet on a work surface, with the shorter end facing you. Lay a sheet of filo lengthways on the baking sheet and brush with melted butter. Top with another sheet and brush with more butter. Take 2 more sheets and turn them so that they are at the 11 o'clock and 5 o'clock positions, brushing each sheet you add with the melted butter. Continue to arrange the sheets in a clockwork fashion, until you have an incrementally overlapping circle shape. Be sure to butter each sheet liberally.

When all the sheets have been used, place the pumpkin mixture in the center and spread out into a circle— leaving a good 2-inch border. Carefully fold the filo sheets over the edge of the pumpkin mixture, allowing most of the center to still be visible. With the remaining butter, generously brush all the edges of the pie and scatter the nigella seeds over. Bake for 25–30 minutes, until the edges are golden and the center is set.

Remove from the oven, drizzle with honey, sprinkle with the remaining oregano and red pepper flakes and set to one side for 5–10 minutes before slicing and serving.

Pea sott' Olio

Frozen peas submerged and cooked in olive oil, garlic and mint, to enjoy barely warm or at room temperature. Serve alongside grilled fish or lamb chops, or piled on to some garlic-rubbed toast slathered with ricotta, diced feta or torn mozzarella.

2¾fl oz/⅓ cup olive oil

2 cloves of garlic, very finely sliced, or 1 shallot, very finely sliced

a small bunch of fresh mint, leaves roughly chopped (use basil if you like)

1lb 2oz/3½ cups frozen peas, thawed

approx. 1 level teaspoon salt, and freshly ground black pepper to taste

grated zest of 1 lemon

Put three-quarters of the oil into a saucepan with the garlic or shallot, mint and peas. Add the salt and pepper, together with about 3 tablespoons of cold water. Cover with a lid and simmer over a moderate heat for about 5 minutes, then remove from the heat and add the lemon zest.

Pour the peas into a wide shallow dish and top with the remaining oil. Check the seasoning and leave to sit for 5 minutes before serving.

Spiced Pea and Filo Parcels

You can't call these samosas. Filo pastry—however brilliant and failsafe—is not the traditional pastry for samosas, nor is baking the usual cooking method. No matter, this recipe is a quick and delicious interpretation of this classic south Asian street food that makes use of freezer staples frozen peas and filo. Terrific straight from the oven, these parcels are also good served at room temperature, making them brilliant for picnics and packed lunches.

1 large potato, about 5½oz, washed and skin left on

salt and freshly ground black pepper

2 tablespoons vegetable oil

1 tablespoon mustard seeds

1 large onion, finely diced

2 cloves of garlic, finely chopped or crushed

2 inches fresh ginger, grated

1 fresh chili, finely chopped (more if you like), or use red pepper flakes

1 tablespoon curry powder (hot or mild), or use garam masala or the punchy baharat blend 2 (see page 164)

3½oz/¾ cup frozen peas, thawed

juice of ½ a lemon

8 filo pastry sheets (you need 2 sheets per 3 samosas—wrap any leftover pastry well and store in the refrigerator to use another time)

3oz/⅓ cup melted butter

approx. 4 teaspoons nigella seeds, to sprinkle between the 2 buttered filo sheets (optional)

MAKES 12 PARCELS

Put the potato into a saucepan and cover with cold water, then add a teaspoon of salt. Bring to the boil and cook until tender. Drain, then leave to cool.

Heat the oil in a frying pan and fry the mustard seeds over a moderate heat until they begin to pop, about a minute. Add the onion, turn down the heat, and continue to cook until soft and translucent, 8–10 minutes. Add the garlic, ginger, chili and spice mix and fry for a further 2 minutes, until fragrant. Add the peas and season with salt and pepper to taste.

Take the skin off the potato—it should slip off. Add the inside of the potato to the peas and mash roughly with a fork or masher. Taste the mix, add the lemon juice, and adjust the seasoning to your liking with salt, pepper and additional chili if necessary.

Preheat the oven to 350°F/gas mark 4 and line a baking tray with baking parchment.

Place 1 sheet of filo on the work surface with the longer edge at the bottom. Brush lightly with melted butter, sprinkle with about 1 teaspoon of nigella seeds, if using, and lay another sheet of filo on top. Cut the pastry lengthways, into 3 slim strips. Place a heaped tablespoon of the pea filling at the far corner of each filo strip and fold diagonally, creating a triangle at the tip of the strip. Continue folding, leaving you with one final join and a complete triangle shape. Repeat with the remaining pastry sheets and filling.

Place on the baking tray and brush with the rest of the butter. Bake for 15–20 minutes, until golden and crisp.

7 VEGETABLES

Using vegetables creatively and with variety is one of my main incentives as a cook. Supported by the pantry, vegetables are the lynchpin to my everyday cooking. I can very easily forgo meat and fish in the food I cook at home if I am well stocked with seasonal vegetables and pantry ingredients are all in keen supply: flours, grains, pasta, noodles and pulses, dairy, various fermented goods and spices give me an endless bill of rapid, delicious combinations. Vegetables are never an afterthought, and onions, garlic too, are always in my pantry.

Olive oil is essential for me where vegetable cookery is concerned. It is the culinary axis between fresh produce and the pantry. My everyday olive oil is of a solid, benchmark quality, nothing terribly posh. Along with salt and pepper, olive oil forms a kitchen triad— it links my daily cooking back to the pantry. These three key ingredients have no place on a shelf or in a cupboard: they are stationed beside my chopping board, next to the stovetop, ready for use at all times. I also tend to have a more specialist, regional extra virgin oil that I use to dress finished dishes. A common mistake is to use olive oil for cooking everything, which means an awful lot of it is wasted. Olive oil has a lower smoke point than other cooking oils and will often burn before it gets to the temperature required to sear or hard-fry ingredients. Common sense must prevail: olive oil is happiest just hot, warm or at room temperature, never at a raging heat. This is why, used to soften so many vegetables over a moderate heat or to dress a dish, olive oil will triumph. Many of my savory recipes begin with an onion and enough olive oil to just cover the base of the saucepan, cooking the onion until soft and translucent. Over a moderate heat, this should take between 8 and 10 minutes, with the onion collapsing in the heat and turning sweet and irreplaceable, but never browning. Likewise, used cold to dress cooked vegetables, pasta, pulses, grains or dribbled over seasoned yogurt, olive oil is alchemy. Depending on the flavors of a dish, i.e. not too assertive, I might choose to use the more expensive extra virgin olive oil here, letting the oil be star of the dish. Not all dishes are flattered by olive oil, however. Sometimes the pepperiness of olive oil needs to be tempered by a neutral oil (vegetable, sunflower or groundnut) in a dressing, so the dish is not so overly olive-y—the leek vinaigrette, for example, on page 229. Some dishes feature so many other flavors in the mix that olive oil just isn't necessary, and inexpensive neutral oil will fit the bill—the Caesar salad (see page 213) is one of these. Liberal in use, but canny in usage, is my approach.

Fresh vegetables invite you to cook and enjoy them as the year unfolds. They are very different in application from the dried and preserved commodities of the pantry, almost all season-less in use. Tomatoes? I would rather use good-quality canned, drained of their juice and seasoned with salt, pepper and olive oil for any cooking requiring whole fresh tomatoes if the season is anything other than summer or early autumn. The recipes in this chapter celebrate fresh vegetables, all bolstered with key pantry ingredients. Marry wintry vegetables with warm robust spice and roasted sourdough, such as in the root vegetable recipe (see page 223), and pair sprightly spring radishes and rhubarb with a young fresh goat's curd, for example. Cooked creatively, with enthusiasm and support from the pantry, a largely vegetable-based diet is no hardship.

PANTRY BASICS

CUPBOARD

olive oil (basic and extra virgin)

neutral oil (vegetable, sunflower or groundnut)

canned plum tomatoes

FRESH

onions

garlic

QUICK VEGETABLES

10fl oz/1¼ cups vinegar—red wine, white wine or cider

7fl oz/¾ cup water

3½oz/½ cup sugar

1 tablespoon Dijon mustard

1 tablespoon mustard seeds

1 teaspoon black peppercorns

1 teaspoon coarse sea salt

a large sprig of thyme

3 bay leaves

2 tablespoons miso paste, light or dark

1lb 7oz assorted vegetables for pickling (see recipe introduction)

MAKES 1LB 7OZ

Two Quick Pickles

Keep these pickles in the refrigerator—their flavor will increase the longer they are kept in the pickle juice. Use the pickling vinegar in salad dressings or in marinades. Use carrots, radishes, celery, cauliflower florets, small turnips, small beets, inner pale cabbage leaves, apples, rhubarb, green beans, bell peppers. Peel where necessary and prepare ingredients in a similar fashion, sliced or diced as bite-sized pieces, no bigger than 5 inches.

Pickle 1: miso and mustard

Combine the vinegar, water, sugar, mustard and seeds, peppercorns, salt, thyme, bay leaves and miso in a big non-reactive pot and bring to the boil, stirring to dissolve the sugar. Remove from the heat and leave to cool.

Prepare the vegetables so that they are roughly equal in size and place them in a wide shallow container so that they are not too on top of each other.

Pour the cold pickling liquid over the vegetables to submerge them. Cover with plastic wrap or a lid and refrigerate the pickles for at least 24 hours before serving, 2–3 days is best. They will keep for up to 2 weeks in the refrigerator.

10fl oz/1¼ cups vinegar—red wine, white wine or cider

10fl oz/1¼ cups water

2¾oz/about ⅓ cup sugar

2 cloves of garlic, peeled and slightly crushed

2 teaspoons fennel seeds

1 heaped teaspoon toasted coriander seeds, bashed a little

1½ tablespoons coarse salt

a large sprig of thyme

3 bay leaves

red pepper flakes, to taste, about ½–1 teaspoon

1lb 7oz assorted vegetables for pickling (see recipe introduction on page 206)

MAKES 1LB 7OZ

Pickle 2: chili and herb

Combine the vinegar, water, sugar, garlic, spices, salt, thyme and bay leaves in a non-reactive saucepan and bring to the boil, stirring well to dissolve the sugar. Remove from the heat and leave to cool.

Prepare the vegetables so that they are roughly equal in size and place them in a wide shallow container so that they are not too on top of each other.

Pour the cold pickling liquid over the vegetables to submerge them. Cover with plastic wrap or a lid and refrigerate the pickles for at least 24 hours before serving, 2–3 days is best. They will keep for up to 2 weeks in the refrigerator.

Runner Beans with Tapenade and New Potatoes

I love tapenade. Salty rich with a piquant capery punch, it is wonderful in this warm potato and bean salad. Chopped ripe cherry tomatoes mixed through would be good here too. Make green tapenade with green olives instead of black, and add a handful of chopped walnuts to the mix if you like.

Cook the potatoes in plenty of boiling salted water for about 15 minutes or until tender, adding the beans for the final 5 minutes of cooking time. Remove from the heat, drain and keep warm.

To make the tapenade, put the olives, garlic, capers and anchovies on a board and chop, or pulse in a processor until you have a coarse paste. Mix in the olive oil.

Toss the tapenade with the warm new potatoes, runner beans and the raw shallots and serve immediately.

1lb 2oz new potatoes, peeled and cut into even-sized pieces

14oz/about 3 cups trimmed and sliced runner beans (use green beans if you prefer)

3½oz/1 cup Kalamata olives, pitted

1 clove of garlic, crushed

1 tablespoon capers

6 anchovy fillets in oil

2–3 tablespoons olive oil

2 shallots or 1 red onion, very thinly sliced

Grilled Green Beans with Feta, Dill and Pine Nuts

14oz green beans, trimmed

3 tablespoons extra virgin olive oil

salt and freshly ground black pepper

juice of ½–1 lemon, to taste

a small bunch of fresh dill, leaves roughly chopped

1¾oz/about ½ cup pine nuts, toasted

3½oz/about ¾ cup crumbled feta cheese (mozzarella is good too)

If you are cooking these beans on an outdoor grill, they can be easier to deal with if you thread them on to a skewer, as they won't fall through the bars of the grill. Simply push a wooden skewer halfway along a bean, tossed already in the oil and pinch of salt, and fill each skewer up with more beans. When grilled, you can remove the beans from the skewer and add the remaining ingredients, or leave on the skewers to dress and serve.

Preheat a grill, griddle pan or heavy frying pan.

Place the green beans in a bowl and toss with 1 tablespoon of the olive oil and a big pinch of salt.

When the grill is hot, arrange the green beans on top and grill for about 3 minutes each side, or until just cooked.

Remove from the heat and transfer to a bowl. Add the lemon juice, chopped dill, remaining olive oil and salt and pepper to taste. Mix well.

Arrange the cooked beans on a big plate and sprinkle with the toasted pine nuts and the feta cheese.

Fennel, Rhubarb, Celery, Radish and Goat's Curd

If you can bear it, use a mandoline here for a uniform and thin slice to the rhubarb, celery and fennel. If you don't have one, or are too terrified of these razor-sharp contraptions, just be sure to slice as evenly as you can. Use feta or mozzarella here instead of the goat's curd if you like—I tend to always have at least one of these three stored in my refrigerator to use in salads such as this one.

Whisk the oil with the lemon juice or vinegar, a big pinch of salt and plenty of black pepper.

Mix the rhubarb and vegetables together and gently toss with the dressing just before serving. Arrange on a wide serving plate and top with blobs of curd cheese and the chopped celery leaf and herbs. Serve immediately.

3 tablespoons olive oil

2 tablespoons lemon juice or wine vinegar

salt and freshly ground black pepper

3 sticks of pinkest rhubarb, trimmed and cut on an angle into ¼-inch slices, tossed with 1 teaspoon superfine sugar

1 large fennel bulb, trimmed and cut into ¼-inch slices

½ a bunch of celery, trimmed and cut on an angle into ¼-inch slices (keep the leaves separate and roughly chop)

1 bunch of radishes, trimmed and cut into ¼-inch slices

7oz/1 cup goat's curd cheese or young goat's cheese

a small bunch of fresh mint, dill or parsley, leaves roughly chopped

Little Gem Caesar

A classic. The ingredients for the dressing all come from the pantry. A good Caesar is a simple Caesar: just three ingredients—crisp crunchy lettuce, toasted bread and thin slivers of Parmesan—bound in the bowl by an intensely savory dressing. Cold roast chicken and chicken skin crackling will work very well here, but don't say I said so.

Preheat the oven to 350°F/gas mark 4.

Whisk together the anchovies, crushed garlic, mustard, lemon juice and egg yolks. Add the oil, drop by drop to start with, then in a very thin stream until thickened, whisking until the dressing is thick and glossy. You can do this by hand in a bowl or use a food processor, but just be sure to add the oil very slowly to begin with so the dressing doesn't split—essentially you are making a mayonnaise here.

Add the Parmesan, then loosen the texture of the dressing with a splash of water or lemon juice to the consistency of heavy cream. Season with salt and pepper to taste and set aside.

Toss the bread with the 3 tablespoons of oil and the bashed whole garlic. Place on a baking tray and season with salt and pepper. Bake for about 10 minutes, until golden and crisp.

In a bowl mix together the lettuce, croutons and dressing. Top with some Parmesan shavings if you like.

6 anchovy fillets in oil, drained and chopped

2 small cloves of garlic, 1 crushed, 1 whole unpeeled and slightly bashed

1 teaspoon Dijon mustard

juice of ½–1 lemon, to taste

2 large egg yolks

3½fl oz/about ⅓ cup vegetable oil, plus 3 tablespoons to cook the croutons

3 tablespoons finely grated Parmesan cheese (and extra to serve as shavings is nice)

salt and freshly ground black pepper

4 thick slices of sourdough or any rustic bread, torn into pieces

3 Little Gem hearts, leaves separated, or use Cos or Romaine if you like

Tomatoes with Lime, Ginger and Tamarind

1lb 12oz mixed size and color ripe tomatoes

salt and freshly ground black pepper

2 tablespoons tamarind paste, shop-bought, or use a pulp block and loosen with a little warm water to a similar amount

½–1 teaspoon red pepper flakes, to taste

juice of 1 lime

1 tablespoon brown sugar

¾ inch fresh ginger, finely grated

1 teaspoon coriander seeds, toasted and finely ground

2fl oz/just under ¼ cup water

2fl oz/just under ¼ cup neutral oil

a small bunch of fresh cilantro, leaves roughly chopped

I buy tamarind in a block as pulp from my local Indian or Turkish grocery store, chopping off what I need and loosening it to a paste by covering it with a little boiling water, then leaving it to sit for 5 minutes before pushing it through a sieve to strain out the pips. But you can buy the ready-made paste in jars. Used to give acidity to a dish, tamarind has a sour-sweet flavour and works well in many Indian, south-east Asian and Middle Eastern dishes. I also like to top up pulp with sparkling water and serve it over ice as a refreshing, fruity drink. In this recipe, the tamarind, ginger and lime balance beautifully with the sweet ripe tomatoes.

Prepare the tomatoes by chopping or slicing them thickly according to shape. Arrange them in a serving dish and season with salt and pepper.

Put the tamarind, red pepper flakes, lime juice, sugar, ginger, ground coriander, water and oil into a jar. Put the lid on and shake vigorously until the dressing emulsifies. Taste the dressing and adjust the seasoning if necessary with more salt, pepper and chili.

Pour the dressing over the salad and add the cilantro. Serve immediately.

Roasted Asparagus, Green Onions and Sesame Seeds

The green onions are so good here, if not even better than the more expensive asparagus. You want your oven to be super-hot, and you should douse the asparagus and green onions with the lemon juice immediately on exit from the oven. The scorched stalks will drink with a thirsty, citrusy gasp. Serve hot or at room temperature.

2 bunches of asparagus, washed if gritty, ends trimmed or snapped and cut to the same size as the asparagus

1 bunch of green onions, trimmed

2 tablespoons olive oil

1 teaspoon sesame oil

salt and freshly ground black pepper

1 clove of garlic, finely chopped

3 tablespoons sesame seeds

juice of ½–1 lemon, to taste

Preheat the oven to 425°F/gas mark 7.

Place the asparagus and green onions in a large bowl and mix in the oils, a big pinch of salt and the garlic. Mix well to combine.

Arrange flat in one layer on a large baking sheet and bake in the very hot oven for 5 minutes, then sprinkle over the sesame seeds and cook for a further 2–5 minutes, until the asparagus is just tender and the green onions have wilted and even singed in places. Remove from the oven and squeeze over the lemon juice, adding more salt and black pepper to your liking.

Arrange on a plate and serve.

Sweet and Sour Pumpkin

This sounds terribly old-fashioned, but don't let that put you off. Served at room temperature, it's the perfect dish to make during the day and leave out of the refrigerator for the flavors to meld. Add the mint just before you plan on serving on its own or as sidekick to roast pork, lamb or grilled steak. Or serve with some garlic-rubbed toast and torn balls of mozzarella. Use the chili and herb quick pickle liquor (see page 208) to add to the pan when you make the syrup, if you like.

3–6 tablespoons olive oil

1 good-sized pumpkin (approx. 1lb 10oz), peeled and cut into ½-inch slices

salt and freshly ground black pepper

6fl oz/¾ cup white wine vinegar (or quick pickle juice, see recipe introduction)

2 cloves of garlic, finely chopped

1 teaspoon superfine sugar

1 small bunch of fresh mint, leaves roughly chopped

Heat a good-sized frying pan with enough oil to fry the pumpkin slices in small batches until bronzed on both sides and easily pierceable with a sharp knife. Season with salt and pepper as you cook each batch of pumpkin, adding a little more oil to the pan as necessary.

With each batch cooked, transfer the pumpkin to a wide flat serving dish and continue cooking the rest.

With the pumpkin all cooked and housed in the serving dish, using the same frying pan because it will hold all the caramelized pumpkin flavor, tip out any excess oil in the pan and add the vinegar along with the chopped garlic and sugar. Bring the vinegar to the boil over a moderate heat and dissolve the sugar. Pour the hot syrup over the cooked pumpkin, leave to cool and scatter over the chopped fresh mint to serve.

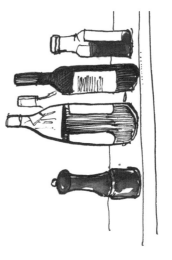

1 large Savoy cabbage, outer
leaves and hard inner core
removed, sliced into approx.
½-inch ribbons

FOR THE PESTO
½ a preserved lemon (see page
284 for homemade), flesh and pith
removed and rind finely chopped

a small bunch of fresh dill, leaves
roughly chopped

a small bunch of fresh flat-leaf
parsley, leaves roughly chopped

1 clove of garlic, finely chopped
or crushed

1¾oz pine nuts, toasted in a dry
frying pan over a moderate heat
until golden brown

2¾fl oz/just under ½ cup olive oil

Savoy Cabbage with
Preserved Lemon, Dill
and Pine Nut Pesto

**Pesto doesn't always have to be the basil version. Here
with preserved lemon and dill, these bold and punchy
flavors are terrific with plain boiled Savoy cabbage.
Serve as a side dish to some grilled pork or chicken,
or piled on to garlic-rubbed toast with some ricotta
for a simple lunch. Experiment—use various cooked
vegetables or grilled meat with this pesto.**

To make the pesto, put the lemon, dill, parsley and
garlic into a food processor and blitz to a rough
green paste.

Add the pine nuts and blitz, retaining some texture to
the nuts.

Add the oil and blitz briefly. Scrape from the blender
into a bowl.

If not using straight away, cover the pesto with extra
olive oil, making sure it is completely submerged. It will
keep well in the refrigerator for up to a week.

Boil the prepared cabbage in plenty of salted boiling
water until tender, about 3–5 minutes. Drain well, then
put the cabbage into a warm serving dish.

Add the pesto to the cooked cabbage and mix well
before serving, reserving a final tablespoon of the pesto
to slick on top.

Fresh Spinach with Avocado, Grapefruit and Poppy Seed Dressing

Poppy seeds are a wonderful ingredient to have in your pantry. Used in this dressing they give a lovely blue-black and peppery freckle to the salad ingredients and contrast beautifully with the avocado and pink grapefruit. Use in pancake batters and cakes, or on mirin-glazed eggplant (see page 231).

1 small red onion, finely sliced

1 tablespoon white wine vinegar or lemon juice

1 tablespoon poppy seeds

1 teaspoon runny honey

1 teaspoon Dijon mustard

3 tablespoons olive oil

½ teaspoon each of salt and freshly ground black pepper

2–3 ripe avocados

7oz/about 4 cups baby spinach leaves, rinsed and dried

2 pink grapefruit, peeled and segmented or sliced into thick rounds (remove as much pith as you can, but don't let it worry you too much; I don't mind it)

Put the onion into a bowl with the vinegar and leave to macerate for 5 minutes. Drain the onion, reserving the vinegar, and put to one side.

Put the vinegar, poppy seeds, honey, mustard, oil, salt and pepper into a jar with a lid and shake to blend and for the flavors to mingle.

Peel, pit and slice the avocados.

Just before serving, place the spinach in a large bowl and toss with half the dressing. Add the avocado, grapefruit and macerated onion and drizzle with the remaining dressing to serve.

Arugula with Cherries, Quick Pickled Shallots and Almonds

Fruit salad served savory. Along with the arugula, radicchio and toasted almonds, the cherries here give a big showy and juicy burst to this pretty salad.

4 medium shallots, thinly sliced

3 tablespoons red wine vinegar

1 small radicchio, shredded

3½oz/about 3 cups arugula

7oz/1⅓ cups cherries, stemmed, pitted and cut in half

6 tablespoons olive oil

1¾oz/⅔ cup flaked almonds, toasted

salt and freshly ground black pepper

Combine the shallots with the red wine vinegar and leave to macerate in a small bowl while you prepare the rest of the ingredients.

In a large bowl or on a plate, combine all the ingredients except the almonds, including the shallots along with their vinegar. Check the salad leaves for seasoning, adjusting with salt and pepper if necessary.

Top with the toasted almonds and serve immediately.

SLOW
VEGETABLES

Roasted Bread and Root Vegetables with Mustard, Cumin and Pumpkin Seeds

Sweet roasted root vegetables earthy with mustard, cumin and pumpkin seeds, here with my all-time favorite, roasted and toasted day-or-two-old bread. Use good rustic crunchy bread; white sliced will never come good in this recipe.

1lb 5oz/about 4 cups chopped mixed root vegetables, approx. ¾-inch pieces

2 onions, red or white, finely sliced

1 teaspoon cumin seeds

2 teaspoons mustard seeds

6 tablespoons olive oil

3 teaspoons runny honey

4 thick slices of sourdough or any rustic bread, torn into pieces about the same size as the vegetables

4 tablespoons pumpkin seeds (or sunflower seeds)

2 tablespoons cider vinegar or red wine vinegar

salt and freshly ground black pepper

a big bunch of fresh flat-leaf parsley, leaves roughly chopped

Preheat the oven to 400°F/gas mark 6.

Toss the root vegetables with the onions, cumin and mustard seeds and 2 tablespoons of olive oil. Roast in the oven for about 40 minutes, until golden. You can remove any of the vegetables that cook more quickly and reserve these on a plate, leaving any stubborn vegetables in the oven to cook for longer. When all the vegetables are cooked, remove and toss them all together with 2 teaspoons of the honey.

While the root vegetables are roasting, toss the bread with 1 tablespoon of olive oil and roast on a separate roasting tray for about 10 minutes. Then add the seeds and bake for a further 5 minutes, until the bread is golden and crisp.

Make the dressing by putting the remaining 3 tablespoons of olive oil, the remaining teaspoon of honey, the vinegar, salt and pepper, to taste, into a jar and shaking vigorously with the lid on to amalgamate.

Put the roasted vegetable mixture and the toasted bread into a large bowl and pour over the dressing. Check the seasoning and add the parsley, mixing well to combine.

Yogurt and Garam Slow-roasted Carrots

Slow-roasting the carrots in a garam-flavored yogurt makes for gorgeous spicy curds clinging to the cooked carrots. This dish looks incredible, with the turmeric oil giving a final flashy streak of color. My refrigerator is never without yogurt. I use it almost daily in many different ways. The turmeric oil is an arresting shade of deep yellow-orange and has a fantastic peppery, mustardy flavor.

2 tablespoons garam masala (though this is equally good with ras al hanout or with either of the baharat blends on page 164)

1 clove of garlic, crushed

7oz/1 cup Greek yogurt

5 tablespoons neutral oil

salt and freshly ground black pepper

1lb 2oz small to medium carrots, trimmed, scrubbed or peeled and halved lengthways

1 large onion, finely sliced

½ level teaspoon ground turmeric

juice of ½–1 lemon, to taste

1 small bunch of fresh cilantro, leaves roughly chopped (use mint if you prefer)

Preheat the oven to 425°F/gas mark 7.

Mix the garam masala with the garlic, half the yogurt and half the oil in a large bowl and season with salt and pepper. Add the carrots and sliced onion and mix well to coat.

Lay the coated carrots and onions on a roasting tray in a single layer and roast for about 25 minutes, or until tender and golden in places.

Meanwhile, add the turmeric to the remaining oil and heat in a small pan over a moderate heat for 1 minute. Remove from the heat and put to one side.

Mix the lemon juice and remaining yogurt with half the chopped herbs, and season with salt and pepper to taste.

Place the cooked carrots (along with any caramelized bits from the pan) on a big plate. Dress with the yogurt and turmeric oil and top with the rest of the chopped herbs.

Cavolo Nero Cooked Slowly with Garlic, Olive Oil and Fennel Seeds

2 bunches of cavolo nero (about 1lb 2oz)

2fl oz/just under ¼ cup extra virgin olive oil, or to taste

2 cloves of garlic, finely chopped

1 teaspoon fennel seeds, crushed

a generous pinch of red pepper flakes

First blanched in boiling water, then cooked again in plenty of olive oil with the garlic, fennel seeds and red pepper flakes, this method of cooking cavolo nero is a winning way to serve this winter green. Goes well with grilled meat or simply piled onto garlic-rubbed toast, with or without some ricotta.

Wash the cavolo nero, strip out the tough stems and roughly chop the leaves.

Cook in boiling water for about 5 minutes, until just tender, then drain well and set aside.

Heat the olive oil in a saucepan over low to medium heat, then add the garlic, fennel seeds and red pepper flakes and fry gently. Add the cavolo nero, then cover and cook for about 10–15 minutes, checking in from time to time, until the cavolo nero is completely soft and tender.

Cauliflower with Green Olives and Almonds

Roasting cauliflower, as if almost to overcook it, gives this brassica a sweet roasted flavor. Salty olives boost the seasoning and the nuts give a welcome crunch.

1lb 2oz/about 4 cups cauliflower, cut into approx. 1-inch florets

2 tablespoons extra virgin olive oil

salt and freshly ground black pepper

2¼oz/ about ½ cup whole almonds, skin on or off as you like, roughly chopped

2¾oz/about ½ cup pitted green olives, roughly chopped

a small bunch of fresh flat-leaf parsley, leaves roughly chopped

juice of ½–1 lemon, to taste

Preheat the oven to 425°F/gas mark 7.

In a shallow baking dish, toss the cauliflower with the oil and season with salt and pepper.

Roast for 20 minutes, or until the cauliflower is tender and golden in places.

Add the almonds and olives and mix together, then roast for a further 5–10 minutes, until the almonds are lightly toasted and the cauliflower is tender. Check the seasoning.

Remove from the oven and place in a serving bowl. Add the parsley and lemon juice and mix well to combine.

Serve warm or at room temperature.

5½oz bacon, cut into ⅝-inch strips

1½ tablespoons butter

1 large onion, finely diced

2 bay leaves

2 cloves of garlic, finely chopped

1 tablespoon caraway seeds

10½oz/about 5 cups finely sliced white cabbage

10½oz/about 2¼ cups potatoes, peeled and cut into ¾-inch dice

1¾ pints/4 cups chicken or vegetable stock

salt and freshly ground black pepper

2¾–3½fl oz/about ⅓ cup pickle juice (see recipe introduction), or to taste

TO SERVE

sour cream or crème fraîche

a generous pinch of paprika, sweet or hot

a small bunch of fresh dill, leaves roughly chopped

Cabbage and Caraway Soup with Pickle Juice and Sour Cream

This is the sort of soup that will take you by surprise. It may not look at all lovely, but one spoonful and I'm fairly sure it is all you will want to eat all winter long. Use the sour brine from shop-bought sour pickled gherkins or cucumbers as the magic ingredient here, giving this hearty soup a beautiful, beguiling taste.

Fry the bacon in the butter until beginning to crisp, about 5 minutes. Reduce the heat to low, add the onion and bay leaves, and cook for 8–10 minutes, stirring from time to time, until the onion is soft and translucent.

Add the garlic and caraway, and cook for 1 minute. Add the cabbage and potatoes and cook for 5 minutes, stirring occasionally.

Add the stock, season with a bit of salt and pepper, bring to the boil and simmer for 20 minutes, until the potatoes are tender.

Blend about 2 cupfuls of the soup in a blender and return the blended soup to the pan of unblended soup. Check the seasoning and add the pickle juice, adding still more if you like.

Serve with a dollop of sour cream, a pinch of paprika and some chopped dill.

Leek Vinaigrette with Grated Egg and Capers

Serve warm or at room temperature. This dressing will also work well with cooked asparagus. I keep salted capers in my refrigerator, covering the required amount with cold water and desalinating them before use—they are more pungent in flavour, but pickled capers are fine to use and will give a more acerbic blast to this dish.

Check that the leeks are thoroughly clean.

Cook the leeks in plenty of salted boiling water with the peppercorns, thyme, garlic and bay leaves for 8–10 minutes, or until tender. Remove from the pan and drain well, then lay the leeks out to drain completely on a clean dish towel. Discard the aromatics.

Put the mustard, vinegar and crème fraîche into a small bowl, add a little salt and pepper to taste and whisk together. Whisk in the oils in a thin stream to emulsify.

Lay the cooked warm leeks on a large plate and spoon over half the dressing. Grate over the hard-boiled eggs with a cheese grater, add the herbs and capers and drizzle over the remaining dressing.

20 small trimmed young leeks, well washed

1 tablespoon whole black peppercorns

a small bunch of fresh thyme

2 cloves of garlic, peeled and lightly bashed

3 bay leaves

FOR THE DRESSING
2 teaspoons Dijon mustard

1 tablespoon white wine vinegar or cider vinegar

2 tablespoons crème fraîche

salt and freshly ground black pepper

2 tablespoons olive oil

3 tablespoons neutral oil

2 eggs, hard-boiled (see page 188)

a small bunch of fresh parsley, dill or tarragon, stalks removed and finely chopped

1 tablespoon capers, rinsed and drained if salted

Japanese Eggplant with Mirin and Sesame or Nasu Dengaku

Try to get hold of pale thin-skinned purple eggplants from an Asian supermarket if you can, though the regular black-skinned variety will work well. The eggplant is glazed and cooked with a strong, salty mix of miso and mirin, flattering the fleshy eggplant like nothing else on earth. I've eaten this dish more than a few times in a well-known Japanese restaurant in London and I think this interpretation of a restaurant classic is spot on.

2 eggplants

neutral oil, to brush the eggplants

3 level tablespoons miso paste, light or dark

4 tablespoons mirin (use sherry with a teaspoon of brown sugar if you don't have mirin)

3 tablespoons sake (or same quantity of sherry preparation as above)

1½–2 teaspoons brown sugar

½–1 inch fresh ginger, finely grated

2 teaspoons sesame seeds, toasted, or use poppy seeds

4–6 green onions, very finely sliced on an angle

½–1 teaspoon red pepper flakes (optional)

Preheat the oven to 350°F/gas mark 4.

Using a vegetable peeler, peel strips of skin off the eggplants, leaving wide stripes. Cut the eggplants in half or into thick ¾-inch rounds. Score criss-cross marks on the flesh of the eggplant and place them flat on a baking sheet. Brush with oil and place them in the hot oven to bake until soft, cooked and golden underneath. In slices this should take about 15 minutes; halves will take a little longer, 20–25 minutes. Remove from the oven and set to one side.

Meanwhile, put the miso, mirin, sake and sugar into a small pan and bring to the boil, then simmer for about 3 minutes until the miso has melted and begun to thicken. Add the grated ginger and stir well, then remove from the heat.

Brush the miso glaze over the cooked eggplant halves or rounds and put the tray back into the oven for 3–5 minutes, until the glaze begins to bubble and caramelize on the eggplants.

Remove from the oven and sprinkle with the sesame seeds, green onions and red pepper flakes if using. Serve immediately or eat just warm.

Baked Zucchini Flowers with Breadcrumbs and Ricotta

Not strictly a pantry-dependent recipe but one that I very much wanted to include in this book. Zucchini flowers should not be considered cheffy, restaurant-only ingredients. Sure enough they are expensive to get hold of, but if you know anyone who grows their own, come summertime they are likely to have an abundance. Lots of chefs and cooks seem to like coating the flowers in a batter before deep-frying them, but I think this masks their gorgeous, dainty, silken texture. Stuff them with ricotta and herbs instead and lay them on a bed of fresh tomato sauce before baking them to a bubble with breadcrumbs (pantry!) and Parmesan. (Having now written this down, if that doesn't sound restaurant-y, I don't know what does...)

Zucchini flowers are best picked on a dry day when they are wide open. Pick them either on stems or with their small zucchini fruit attached. You'll need about 8 for this recipe. Pinch off the sepals and the stamen straight away before the flower begins to close, which it does soon after it is picked. Any zucchini flowers that have already closed should be opened very gently, as the petals may be entwined and are prone to rip.

FOR THE FRESH TOMATO SAUCE
1lb 2oz ripe tomatoes

1 tablespoon olive oil

2 cloves of garlic, finely chopped

salt, freshly ground black pepper and/or red pepper flakes, to taste

a large bunch of fresh herbs—basil, parsley, oregano, marjoram—or a good-sized bunch of thyme

FOR THE STUFFED FLOWERS
7oz/1 cup ricotta

1oz/about ½ cup freshly grated Parmesan or Pecorino cheese, plus a little extra for sprinkling on top

reserved herbs from the tomato sauce, finely chopped

2 zucchini, finely diced and lightly fried in a little olive oil to still retain some bite—about 2 minutes over a high heat to color

salt, freshly ground black pepper and/or red pepper flakes, to taste

8 zucchini flowers, prepared as directed opposite

2fl oz/¼ cup heavy cream

1oz/about ½ cup breadcrumbs, lightly toasted

First skin the tomatoes for the sauce. To do this, slit the side of each tomato skin with a sharp knife, then put them into a bowl and cover with boiling water. Leave for under 1 minute or, if the tomatoes are small, 15–30 seconds, then drain and slip off the skins.

Remove the seeds and the juice from the tomatoes. It's best to do this over a sieve positioned over a bowl, collecting the strained juice as you work. Roughly chop the skinned flesh.

Warm the olive oil in a pan and add the garlic. Soften a little without coloring for 1–2 minutes, then add the chopped tomatoes.

Cook over a moderately high heat until the flavor is concentrated but the sauce remains fresh-tasting, about 5 minutes. Add the strained tomato juice midway through the cooking, mixing well.

Remove from the heat and season to taste with salt, black pepper and/or red pepper flakes. Chop half the herbs and add to the tomato sauce, keeping the remaining half for stuffing the zucchini flowers. Set the sauce aside.

Preheat the oven to 400°F/gas mark 6.

In a bowl combine the ricotta, Parmesan, remaining herbs, cooked zucchini and some seasoning.

Open the zucchini flower petals and stuff the flowers with the ricotta mixture, pushing the mixture into the center with a teaspoon. Don't overfill them. Twist each flower gently to close.

Pour the tomato sauce into a wide shallow baking dish and gently flatten each stuffed flower a bit as you lay them in the sauce.

Pour the heavy cream over the stuffed flowers, then scatter over the breadcrumbs and an extra handful of grated Parmesan.

Cook in the oven for 10–15 minutes, until bubbling at the edges and hot all the way through. Serve immediately.

Cianfotta

I am in the habit of calling this recipe potato ratatouille. Originating, some say, in Naples, is a bold interpretation of a classic French ratatouille. Potatoes give ballast to the vegetables and the vinegar works a treat, splashed over as the potatoes drain. Chili ramps up flavor and, as ever, an exact olive oil measurement is a tricky thing, especially when cooking eggplants, which soak up olive oil like a sponge does water. Pantry, certainly, showcasing here the ever-reliable canned tomatoes among others.

1 large red onion, finely chopped

6 tablespoons olive oil

2 large potatoes, peeled and cut into 1¼-inch cubes

approx. 5 drops/½ teaspoon red wine vinegar, to taste

1 eggplant, cut into 1¼-inch cubes

2 cloves of garlic, finely chopped

½ teaspoon red pepper flakes, or more to taste

1 red or yellow bell pepper, diced

1 x 14oz can of plum tomatoes, drained of juice (keep the juice for another time)

salt and freshly ground black pepper

1½oz/⅓ cup olives, black or green, pitted and roughly chopped

a small bunch of fresh marjoram, oregano, parsley or basil, leaves roughly chopped

Fry the onion in 2 tablespoons of olive oil in a medium saucepan over a medium heat for 8–10 minutes, until soft and translucent.

Boil the potatoes in plenty of salted water until tender and cooked through, then drain. Add the vinegar to the hot potatoes.

While the onions and potatoes are cooking, fry the eggplant in a frying pan in small batches in the remaining olive oil until softened and golden, about 5–7 minutes, adding more oil if required.

Add the garlic, red pepper flakes and bell pepper to the softened onion and cook for 3 minutes, until the bell pepper starts to soften. Stir every so often.

Add the drained whole tomatoes, season with salt and pepper, then cook for 20 minutes to make a rich thick sauce.

Add the cooked eggplant and vinegar-doused potatoes to the tomato pan. Stir and cook for 3–4 minutes for the flavors to combine.

Remove from the heat and stir in the olives, together with a few drops of vinegar to sharpen the flavor. Taste and add more salt, pepper, red pepper or vinegar if you think it needs it. Finally add the herbs and serve.

8 MEAT AND FISH

There are usually additional guests at my table come lunch or supper and I enjoy cooking the sort of food that can feed many. For me that doesn't necessarily mean a vast quantity of meat. Rather, I relish a sense of frugality, when the meat purchased is bolstered by additional ingredients, stretching the quantity, filling more mouths than if it had just been cooked plain and unadorned. I tend to buy the best quality my budget can afford, championing cheaper cuts, serving smaller portions of meat supported with generous portions of vegetables, pulses or grains. Furnished with an inspiring array of ingredients, look to your cupboards and cold store to fortify the more expensive ingredients you buy. Feeding a crowd of friends and family requires clever cooking, with an eye on flavor as well as economy.

I'm reminded of a holiday in northern Cyprus a few years ago, when I met Yildiz, a Turkish-Cypriot friend of a friend. We arranged to spend the day cooking, and she agreed to teach me a traditional Turkish dish. Together we bundled into my tiny hire car, complete with her teenage daughter and my daughter, then only about 18 months old. We drove to the nearby market on narrow dusty roads lined with wild rosemary bushes. The market was a gorgeous gallimaufry of bright, fresh produce, long, cronky wooden trestle tables weighed down with purple and black eggplants, tomatoes, cabbages, onions, wild oregano, potatoes and garlic.

A spice merchant was selling red pepper flakes in tall fragile pyramids, Aleppo and Urfa, sweet-smelling and oily to the touch. To feed her family of six and mine, then three, Yildiz bought just over two pounds of lamb mince. I sat on a stool in her kitchen, drinking syrupy shots of Turkish coffee, scribbling notes and watching as she made one small bag of mince swell to feed a party of nine. Dipping in and out of her pantry, a small room adjacent to the kitchen and open on to the courtyard, out came rice, spice, a string of onions and a cooking pot. As with most savory recipes, Yildiz began with some onions, cooking them to sweet dissolution. The mince was browned in small batches as the rice cooked. Cabbage leaves were blanched. The components of the dish began to amass and the kitchen smelt outrageously good, of food I could not wait to eat.

I still have my notes from that day, and amid my distracted scrawl (I couldn't take my eyes off the cooking), I've noted how Yildiz added each ingredient, eking out flavor, before adding the next. The significance of the pantry is paramount to this recipe. The quantity of mince was not large, but along with the onions, spice, rice and herbs, the synergy of this dish was impressive and utterly delicious. It is a culinary yardstick that I now always try to copy; making more of less. (Yildiz's recipe, or my transcription of it, is on page 242.)

Like meat, good fresh fish caught sustainably, mostly on day boats, can also be pricey. I have lived by the sea and appreciate the fish I've bought from the quayside, so fresh their frames are still tight with rigor mortis. Older fish will lose the rigor, turning limp as the nerves and muscles contract. I live in a city now and prefer to buy fish when I am back near the sea, where the fish shops are many and the fish have not long been out of the water. This moderation makes sense to me, especially when considering some fish stocks are catastrophically low and in need of conservation. As with meat, making more of less is a maxim I live by when cooking with fish.

Linguine con vongole embodies the pantry and represents the very best of cooking: buying a favorite ingredient and making use of it alongside other more utilitarian, everyday ingredients to produce something special. The talent in cooking like the Neapolitan grandmother I mentioned back in my introduction on page 14—heroic, munificent, even a little bit scary (a bit like some chefs I suppose?)—is to spot an enticing ingredient, know you want to cook with it and have the resources back home in your kitchen to make it the best it can be. The art of a good pantry facilitates this. While the clams she cooked on that day are memorable as sweet tiny punctuations to the pasta, I am not so sure that what I didn't love more was the tangle of chili-spiked, parsley-flecked linguine.

It would be odd to write about fish and the role of the pantry and not mention salted anchovies. So, I will finish here with the importance of these slim, firm juicy fillets have to the kitchen and to cooking. With a complex, transformational flavor and unbeatable culinary versatility, anchovies in their many guises are a crucial ingredient. Draped whole over tomatoes, bell peppers, lettuce, hard-boiled eggs, steak, pizza, roast meats, they give seasoning and balance. Chopped and mixed through pasta, potatoes baked with cream, tomato sauces or meat cooking juices, they can add a gorgeous boost to the finished flavor of a sauce or dish. Blitzed in herb sauces or butters they give a glorious and unmistakable pungency. Pounded with softened garlic and amalgamated with melted butter and olive oil, bagna cauda (see page 264), served just warm, is a sauce so astonishing in flavor that trailing raw sticks of vegetables or crusty bread through it is an evening well spent.

PANTRY BASICS

canned anchovies

coconut milk

chicken stock cubes or bouillon

runny honey

piquillo pepper

salted capers

mustard (Dijon and grain)

preserved lemons (see page 284)

dry white wine

Spiced Lamb and Rice Cabbage Leaves

Herewith Yıldız's legendary Cypriot lamb recipe (see pages 237–8).

2 medium onions, finely diced

4–6 tablespoons olive oil

3 cloves of garlic, finely sliced

14oz minced lamb

5½oz/¾ cup Basmati rice

a small bunch of fresh flat-leaf parsley, leaves roughly chopped

grated zest of 1 lemon and juice of ½ lemon

1 teaspoon ground cinnamon

1 teaspoon ground allspice

1 tablespoon dried oregano

1 teaspoon sumac (optional)

salt and freshly ground black pepper

1 large Savoy cabbage, leaves separated

1 x 14oz can of plum tomatoes, drained of their juice

7fl oz/just under 1 cup chicken stock or boiling water

1½oz/just under ¼ cup butter

TO SERVE

9oz/1¼ cups Greek yogurt, seasoned with salt

a small bunch of fresh dill, leaves roughly chopped

approx. 1 tablespoon dried mint

approx. 1 teaspoon red pepper flakes

the remaining ½ lemon, cut into wedges

SERVES 4–6

Fry the onions in 2 tablespoons of olive oil in a good heavy-bottomed saucepan for about 8–10 minutes, until soft and translucent. Add the garlic and continue to cook for 2 minutes more. Put to one side in a large mixing bowl.

Add another 2 tablespoons of olive oil and fry the lamb, in batches if you have an especially small pan, until nicely browned. Add the cooked lamb to the reserved onion mix, and repeat until all the mince is browned off.

Meanwhile, boil the kettle. Put 1 tablespoon of oil into another saucepan that has a tight-fitting lid. When the oil is hot, add the rice and give it a brisk stir for 30 or so seconds, to coat all the grains in the hot oil. Add 10fl oz/1¼ cups of boiling water, let the rice bubble up, then put the lid on the pan. Turn down the heat to a simmer and cook until the water has completely evaporated and the rice is cooked. Remove from the heat and leave to rest for 5 minutes.

Add the cooked rice to the minced lamb and onions, then add the parsley, lemon zest, cinnamon, allspice, oregano and sumac, if using, and give the ingredients a good and thorough mix—with your hands is best. Season with salt and pepper to taste.

In a large pan of salted boiling water, cook the bigger cabbage leaves a couple at a time until tender, about 2 minutes for the outer dark green leaves, less for the pale inner ones. Remove with a slotted spoon and leave to drain well.

CONTINUED

CONTINUED

When the leaves are cool enough to handle, remove any of the larger firm cores from the tough outer leaves, as these will hinder rolling and make for a less flexible leaf.

Preheat the oven to 350°F/gas mark 4.

Place about 2 heaped tablespoons of the lamb mix in the center of each cabbage leaf and roll it up like a fat cigar. Place the cabbage rolls seam side down in a large baking dish or lidded casserole, side by side in one layer.

Tear or chop the drained whole tomatoes into smaller pieces and pop these in among the cabbage rolls.

Heat the stock or boiling water and pour it evenly over the cabbage rolls. Cover with foil or a lid and put into the oven for 45–60 minutes.

Meanwhile, melt the butter over a moderate heat in a small saucepan until nut-brown sediments begin to fall away to the bottom of the pan. Add the lemon juice and stir well. Set to one side.

Remove from the oven and let it rest for around 15 minutes. This dish is best eaten warm, not piping hot. When ready to serve, spoon the seasoned yogurt over the cabbage rolls, pour over the browned butter, and sprinkle with dill, dried mint and red pepper flakes, to taste. Serve with the remaining lemon half, cut into wedges.

Pork, Ricotta and Lemon Meatballs

Ricotta lends a creamy softness to the pork mince here. It also extends the quantity of meat. As nothing beats a cold meatball served the next day wedged in some crusty bread with some lettuce and tomato (and absolutely do add some of the quick pickled vegetables on page 206), don't feel that all the meatballs need eating in the one sitting.

1lb 2oz minced pork

1 clove of garlic, finely chopped

1 large onion, ½ coarsely grated, ½ finely diced

grated zest and juice of 1 lemon

a small sprig of fresh thyme, leaves roughly chopped

1½ teaspoons fennel seeds, toasted and lightly crushed

3½oz/½ cup ricotta

1¾oz/1 cup fresh white breadcrumbs

salt and freshly ground black pepper

2–3 tablespoons olive oil

3½fl oz/just under ½ cup heavy cream or crème fraîche

pasta, to serve

Parmesan cheese, to serve

Mix the pork, garlic, grated onion, lemon zest, thyme, fennel seeds, ricotta and breadcrumbs with ½ teaspoon of salt and lots of pepper. Form the mix into about 16 balls, about the size of a ping-pong ball.

Heat the oil in a large non-stick pan on a medium-high heat and add enough oil to fry the meatballs for about 7 minutes, turning a few times, until golden-brown all over (they should all fit in the pan, but cook them in batches if need be). Remove from the pan and set to one side.

Add any remaining oil to the pan along with the diced onion and fry for 8–10 minutes, until the onion is soft and translucent. Stir in the cream and about 2½–3½fl oz/about ⅓ cup of cold water. Bring to a simmer, add the lemon juice, salt and black pepper to taste, then add the meatballs and cook for a further 3 or 4 minutes, stirring often, until the meatballs are cooked through and the sauce has thickened.

Meanwhile cook some pasta — spaghetti or short and shapely—as per the packet instructions. Drain, then add the meatballs and sauce to the cooked pasta. Serve with plenty of freshly grated Parmesan.

4 tablespoons olive oil

1 onion, finely diced

1¾oz/1 cup fresh breadcrumbs

approx. 4oz/¾ cup dried peaches, finely sliced or chopped

a small sprig of fresh thyme, leaves roughly chopped

sea salt and freshly ground black pepper

5lb pork belly, boned, skin on

SERVES 4–6

Porchetta with Dried Peach and Thyme

Dried fruit works brilliantly in stuffings, and peach and pork is a beautiful combination. Here the dried peach is surrounded by the rolled belly and plumps up in all the juices as the joint cooks. Serve with green vegetables and roast potatoes or soft polenta, as you like.

Heat the oven to 425°F/gas mark 7.

Heat 1 tablespoon of the oil in a small frying pan. Add the onion and cook until soft and translucent, about 8–10 minutes. Tip the cooked onion into a small mixing bowl and add the breadcrumbs, peaches and thyme. Season with salt and pepper.

Using a sharp knife or a clean Stanley knife, score the pork belly skin at ¾-inch intervals in a criss-cross fashion. Rub 1 tablespoon of sea salt over the skin, then turn the belly over and season with salt and pepper. Arrange the stuffing down the center of the meat lengthways.

Roll the belly tightly, securing the sides neatly together with kitchen string. Put the tied pork belly on a wire rack in a roasting tin.

Roast the pork in the center of the oven for 30 minutes.

Turn the oven down to 350°F/gas mark 4 and continue cooking for 2–2½ hours. If the skin hasn't crisped enough by then, turn the oven back up to 425°F/gas mark 7 and crisp the skin for a further 20 minutes, taking care to not burn it.

Remove the meat from the oven and leave the joint to rest in a warm place for 15 minutes or so before carving.

Pork Chops with Rhubarb, Honey, Ginger and Hazelnuts

Honey, ginger and hazelnuts—all from the pantry— make these pork chops very special indeed. Bashing the meat tenderizes it and cuts the cooking time on these chops. The rhubarb can be prepared in advance and warmed through before serving. Grill or pan-fry as you like, finishing off in a hot oven if the chops are especially hefty. Serve with soft polenta, roasted potatoes or some cooked barley, spelt or farro.

4 x 1¼-inch thick bone-in pork chops

3 tablespoons vegetable oil

1 teaspoon ground ginger

4 tablespoons honey (or use maple syrup)

salt and freshly ground black pepper

1oz/about ¼ cup hazelnuts, finely chopped or crushed

10½oz rhubarb, cut into 1¼ inch pieces

Place the pork chops between two sheets of plastic wrap or baking parchment and, using a rolling pin, pound the fleshy part down to flatten slightly.

Mix together 2 tablespoons of vegetable oil, half the ginger, 3 tablespoons of the honey, 1 teaspoon of salt and 2 tablespoons of the hazelnuts and rub over both sides of the pork. Refrigerate for at least 2 hours (overnight or throughout the day is best).

When ready to cook the pork, preheat the grill or pan to a medium-high heat.

Put the rhubarb into a saucepan with the remaining tablespoon of honey, the remaining ½ teaspoon of ginger and 2 tablespoons of water and cook over a low heat until tender, about 6–10 minutes. Season the rhubarb with a bit of salt and pepper and keep warm.

Grill the pork chops on one side for 4–6 minutes, then turn over and grill on the other side for a further 4–6 minutes, until caramelized and cooked through. Remove from the grill and rest for 5 minutes.

Serve the chops on the bone, or cut the meat off the bone into slices. Serve the meat sitting on a puddle of warm rhubarb, along with any of the meat resting juices. Scatter with the remaining hazelnuts and serve.

Jerk Chicken

Proper jerk chicken is barbecued long and slow, starting off over a high heat and moving out along the grill to cook at a lower heat until soft and tender. This takes some skill, and not least a really efficient outdoor grill. This method first cooks the marinated chicken in the oven and uses a hot pan to sear and color the cooked meat. Eat with rice and peas (cooked kidney or pinto beans mixed through cooked rice).

1 teaspoon ground allspice

1 teaspoon black peppercorns, roughly cracked

½ teaspoon ground cinnamon

½ teaspoon freshly grated nutmeg

a small bunch of fresh thyme, leaves roughly chopped

2 fresh bay leaves

½ a bunch of green onions, trimmed and chopped

2 Scotch bonnet chilies, finely chopped (take a lot of care when handling these—rubber gloves are helpful, and removing the seeds will reduce some of their heat)

1 tablespoon dark brown sugar

½ teaspoon salt

2 tablespoons dark soy sauce

juice of 1 lime

4 large chicken legs, skin on and slashed with a knife to the bone

neutral oil to sear the chicken

Blend the spices in a food processor along with the thyme, bay leaves, green onions, chilies, sugar, salt, soy sauce and lime juice.

Pour the marinade into a bowl and add the chicken, massaging it deep into the incisions in the meat. Try to get some of the marinade in under the skin too. Cover and leave to marinate in the refrigerator for at least 4 hours—overnight or throughout the day is best.

Preheat the oven to 350°F/gas mark 4. Place the chicken legs skin side up on a baking tray lined with baking parchment, and cover them with foil. Cook the chicken for about 45 minutes to 1 hour, until cooked through.

Heat a griddle or frying pan on a high heat. Add a dash of neutral oil and the cooked chicken, and sear the meat on both sides until charred and crisp in places.

Remove from the heat and serve immediately.

West African Groundnut Stew

Groundnuts, or peanuts, feature often in West African cooking. Cooked with gingery tomato paste and spices, the accompanying peanut 'broth' has a mellow but fiery warmth. Serve with plain rice and chopped banana (trust me); the hard-boiled eggs are optional, but worth their weight in gold in this recipe.

Season the chicken with half the salt and some freshly ground black pepper. Heat 2 tablespoons of oil in a large saucepan over a medium heat and add the chicken to the pan. Increase the temperature and stir well to ensure you seal the thighs on both sides. Once they are gently browned all over, remove and set to one side on a plate.

Add the remaining 2 tablespoons of oil to the pan and fry the ginger, onion and red pepper flakes until soft, about 8–10 minutes. Add the spices and 1 teaspoon of black pepper and cook until fragrant, for about 1 minute. Add the tomato paste and cook, stirring, until it begins to lightly caramelize, about 3 minutes.

Add the canned tomatoes and the remaining salt and cook for about 10 minutes, to reduce a little, then stir in the peanut butter and return the chicken to the pan along with 1¼ pints/3 cups of water. Bring to the boil, then reduce the heat to medium-low and cook for about 45 minutes to 1 hour, or until the chicken is cooked through and tender.

Meanwhile cover the eggs with cold water in a saucepan and bring to the boil—time the eggs for 6 minutes from coming to the boil, then remove from the heat and leave in the water until cool enough to peel and halve. Add the eggs to the groundnut stew in the final 5 minutes of cooking time, to warm through in the peanut sauce.

Remove from the heat and check the seasoning, adding more salt and pepper where necessary. Serve the groundnut stew strewn with the sliced banana and chili, peanuts and cilantro.

1lb 5oz bone-in chicken thighs, skinned

1 teaspoon salt

freshly ground black pepper

4 tablespoons vegetable oil

2 inches fresh ginger, finely grated

1 large onion, finely diced

1–2 teaspoons red pepper flakes, to taste

1 teaspoon ground coriander

1 teaspoon ground turmeric

1 teaspoon cumin seeds, toasted and ground

2 tablespoons tomato paste

1 x 14oz can of plum tomatoes

7oz/just under 1 cup peanut butter, smooth or crunchy and unsweetened, or make your own (see page 286)

4 eggs, or as many as you want to cook (optional)

TO SERVE
1 or 2 bananas, sliced into rounds

1 fresh red chili, finely sliced

1¾oz/½ cup roasted salted peanuts, roughly chopped

a small bunch of fresh cilantro, leaves roughly chopped

Fesenjan Chicken

This is an Iranian chicken stew or casserole. Absolutely worth its weight in gold in pantry terms, it is flavored with pomegranate molasses and ground walnuts. Intensely fruity, fesenjan is best served with some plain boiled rice.

Season the chicken on both sides with salt and freshly ground black pepper.

Heat the oil in a large saucepan over a medium heat and add the chicken. Increase the temperature and stir well to ensure you seal the chicken thighs on both sides. Once they are gently browned, remove from the pan and set to one side on a plate.

Add the onions to the same pan and cook until soft and translucent, about 8–10 minutes.

Add the ground walnuts and spices and cook for 1 minute more.

Add the stock or water to the pan, then return the chicken thighs and bring the mixture to a gentle simmer. Cover and cook for 45 minutes over a low heat.

Add the honey and pomegranate molasses and stir well, then cook over a low heat for about another hour, stirring thoroughly every 20 minutes to ensure the walnuts do not stick to the base of the pan.

Serve with the pomegranate seeds and crushed walnuts sprinkled on top.

8 chicken thighs, bone in and skin removed

salt and freshly ground black pepper

2 tablespoons vegetable or olive oil

2 large onions, finely diced

14oz/about 3½–4 cups walnuts, finely ground in a food processor (keep back 1½oz/⅓ cup to sprinkle just crushed on top of the cooked stew)

½ teaspoon ground turmeric

½ teaspoon ground cinnamon

⅙–¼ of a nutmeg, freshly grated

1¾ pints/4 cups chicken stock or water

3 tablespoons honey

7fl oz/just under 1 cup pomegranate molasses

1 pomegranate, seeds only, to garnish (optional)

3 shallots, roughly chopped

5 cloves of garlic, roughly chopped

2 inches fresh ginger, grated

1 teaspoon ground turmeric

4-6 fresh red bird's-eye chilies, or 1 tablespoon red pepper flakes (or more or less to taste)

3 tablespoons vegetable oil

2 lemongrass stalks, sliced lengthways and bruised slightly with the back of a knife or a rolling pin

6 kaffir lime leaves

2 or 3 cloves, ground

1 star anise

1 cinnamon stick

1lb 5oz braising steak, cut into 1¼-inch cubes

1 x 14fl oz can of coconut milk

1 tablespoon tamarind pulp (seedless)

1 teaspoon salt, to taste

1 teaspoon palm sugar, or use white sugar

1¾oz/about ¾ cup coconut flakes or shavings

a small bunch of fresh cilantro, leaves roughly chopped

Beef Rendang

Caramelized spiced beef with coconut milk and toasted coconut shavings—this is an impressive curry to serve alongside sticky or plain rice and a cucumber salad dressed with salt and lime juice. Use beef shin, short rib or cheek instead of braising steak if you like, adding a touch more water as you cook and lengthening the cooking time by an extra 45 minutes or so.

Blend the shallots, garlic, ginger, turmeric and red chilies to a smooth paste.

Heat the vegetable oil in a large frying pan. Over a low heat, gently fry the paste for about 10 minutes.

Add the lemongrass, kaffir lime leaves, ground cloves, star anise and cinnamon stick. Turn up the heat to moderate and add 3½fl oz/⅓ cup of water, then bring to a simmer and gently cook until completely dry and sticky, with all the water absorbed.

Add the beef pieces and cook gently for 10 minutes. Add the coconut milk, tamarind, salt and sugar. Simmer for 45 minutes to 1¼ hours, on a low to moderate heat, until you have a dark brown rich-tasting curry sauce and the beef is tender. Add a tablespoon of water here and there throughout the cooking process if the pan gets too dry. Check for seasoning, adding more salt or sugar to taste.

In a small frying pan over a moderate heat, dry-fry the coconut until it is light brown.

Serve the curry with the toasted coconut and cilantro sprinkled over, and with cooked rice on the side.

Seared Steak and Harissa Sandwich

Harissa is a blend of chili, garlic, olive oil and spices. Here I've added piquillo peppers to the mix, lending a sweet silkiness to this North African condiment. I often make enough harissa to serve over a good few days; it keeps well in the refrigerator covered with a little olive oil. It goes well with roasted meat and fish, and added to stews or mixed through with chopped hard-boiled egg; it is a delicious seasoning to have to hand in your refrigerator.

1lb 5oz rump steak (or use lamb neck fillet), cut into 4 thin steaks

2 tablespoons vegetable oil, for frying

FOR THE HARISSA

3½oz fresh red chilies, stems removed, halved lengthways and seeds removed (wear rubber gloves if you like)

6 jarred piquillo peppers

1 teaspoon cumin, toasted and ground

1 teaspoon paprika

1 teaspoon coriander, toasted and ground

1 teaspoon caraway, toasted and ground (optional)

2 cloves of garlic, peeled

2 teaspoons tomato paste, or use equivalent amount of sun-dried tomatoes

2 teaspoons red wine vinegar, or more to taste

salt

4 tablespoons extra virgin olive oil

To make the harissa, put all the ingredients apart from the olive oil into a blender or food processor and blend until smooth, then add 3 tablespoons of the olive oil in a stream until fully combined.

Taste and season with more salt if required. Harissa keeps well in the refrigerator, covered with the remaining tablespoon of olive oil to seal.

Mix together all the ingredients for the marinade, then add the steaks and leave to marinate in the refrigerator for a few hours (but no longer than 8). Remove the meat from the marinade, strain it, reserving the marinade, and keep everything to one side.

Mix a generous amount of the harissa into the yogurt or mayonnaise, to taste, to make a dressing. You want it to be quite perky.

Warm the rolls in the oven or under a grill, and cut them in half.

Heat a heavy-based frying pan until very hot, then add the oil and fry the meat very quickly, about 1–2 minutes each side, according to how pink you like it. Remove the meat from the pan and put to one side.

CONTINUED

Add the strained onions from the marinade to the still hot pan with a pinch of salt and fry for a minute, then add the marinade juices and let it bubble and reduce a little. Pour the pan juices over the top halves of the bread rolls.

Put the lettuce leaves on the bottom halves of the rolls, add a big dollop of harissa dressing, then slice the meat and add to the rolls. Put the tops on and eat immediately.

FOR THE MARINADE
1 onion, thinly sliced

1 clove of garlic, roughly chopped

½ teaspoon red pepper flakes

1 tablespoon chopped parsley

1 teaspoon dried oregano

2 tablespoons red wine

3 tablespoons olive oil

freshly ground black pepper

TO SERVE
6 tablespoons plain yogurt or mayonnaise

4 large crusty rolls

lettuce leaves, Little Gem, Cos or arugula

Seared Beef with Pine Nuts and Buttermilk Dressing

Serving steak quick-seared, pink and juicy, cut into fat ribbons, can extend the quantity of the steak you buy. One steak can feed two, two steaks can feed four and so on. Buttermilk, or ranch, dressing is knockout with a steak. The buttermilk lends a sour creamy tang, with the mustard and herbs ramping up flavor.

FOR THE DRESSING

7fl oz/just under 1 cup buttermilk (or use sour cream or crème fraîche, let down with a little milk)

3½oz/½ cup mayonnaise, bought or homemade

a small bunch of soft fresh herbs (any or a combination of tarragon, dill, parsley or chives), leaves finely chopped

1 clove of garlic, crushed

1 tablespoon Dijon mustard

salt and freshly ground black pepper

FOR THE SALAD

1lb 5oz steak (rump, sirloin, rib-eye or bavette)

a little cooking oil

1½oz/about ½ cup pine nuts

4 Little Gem lettuces, leaves separated, washed and dried

6 green onions, finely sliced on an angle

a small bunch of fresh flat-leaf parsley, leaves roughly chopped

Combine all the ingredients for the dressing with salt and pepper to taste in a jar and shake vigorously. Taste for seasoning and keep to one side.

Get a griddle, frying pan or outdoor grill very hot. Rub the steaks all over with a little cooking oil and season well with salt. Cook the steak to your liking—I like mine to be a little pink on the inside and would cook an 8oz steak for about 3 minutes each side, resting it well before cutting.

Toast the pine nuts in a dry frying pan over a moderate heat until golden brown.

On a serving plate, arrange the lettuce, green onions and parsley.

Cut the rested steak into thick ribbons and arrange over the salad ingredients. Add the buttermilk dressing, scatter with the pine nuts and serve immediately.

Shrimp Baked with Tomato and Feta

Feta bakes beautifully, as do shrimp, and the best thing about this dish is having the garlicky, lemony shrimp juices to swoop through with some crusty bread. A versatile cheese, feta is a reliable refrigerator staple; the shrimp are more of a luxury.

9oz firm feta cheese

24 good-sized raw shrimp, peeled and deveined

7oz ripe cherry tomatoes or halved vine tomatoes (or use canned tomatoes drained of their juice and seasoned with salt and pepper)

grated zest and juice of 1 large lemon

1 clove of garlic, finely chopped or crushed

2½fl oz/⅓ cup olive oil, plus extra to serve

a good pinch of red pepper flakes

1 teaspoon dried oregano

salt and freshly ground black pepper

2 tablespoons chopped fresh dill

crusty bread, to serve

Preheat the oven to 400°F/gas mark 6.

Break the feta into large pieces and place in a large shallow baking dish.

Toss the shrimp with the tomatoes, lemon zest and juice, garlic, olive oil, red pepper flakes, oregano and salt and pepper to taste.

Spoon the shrimp mixture over the feta and bake for 15 minutes, until the prawns are opaque and cooked through.

Scatter over the dill, drizzle with a little more olive oil and serve immediately, with plenty of crusty bread for mopping up the juices.

Clam Picada

From Catalonia, a picada is a combination of pounded nuts and crusty bread used to thicken and flavor a broth or liquid. Made here with almonds, garlic and fried bread, the picada is added to the clam and sherry cooking juices. You can experiment with different nuts if you like—hazelnuts or walnuts are good—or add a picada to other dishes, such as chicken cooked in stock, or various soupy shellfish dishes. What you have is a punchy, highly flavored ingredient to thicken and invigorate a cooking broth.

Wash the clams in plenty of cold water, discarding any that don't close when tapped on a surface or that have cracked or broken shells.

Dry-roast the almonds for 2 minutes in a frying pan over a moderate heat or in a hot oven, and put to one side to cool. Using the same frying pan, fry the bread with 2 tablespoons of the olive oil for about 3 minutes, until crisp and golden brown.

Use a food processor to blend the roasted almonds, roughly chopped garlic, parsley, fried bread and 2 tablespoons of olive oil into a coarse paste, then put to one side.

Place a large pan that has a lid on the heat and add the remaining 2 tablespoons of olive oil and the sliced garlic. Cook for 1 minute—do not let the garlic brown. As soon as the garlic is fragrant, add the clams and the sherry, cover the pan and cook until the clams have just opened, about 3 minutes.

Remove the pan from the heat, remove the clams with a slotted spoon and keep them to one side. Add the picada to the pan and stir into the cooking juices to thicken them. Return the clams to the pan and check the seasoning.

Serve immediately, with crusty bread.

2lb 4oz clams

2¾oz/about ½ cup skinned whole almonds, roughly chopped

6 tablespoons olive oil

4 slices of crusty white bread, crusts off and torn into 1-inch pieces

4 cloves of garlic, 2 thinly sliced and 2 roughly chopped

a small bunch of fresh flat-leaf parsley, leaves roughly chopped

2½fl oz/⅓ cup dry sherry (fino or manzanilla is best, or use white wine)

salt and freshly ground black pepper

crusty bread, to serve

Mussels with Piquillo Peppers, Capers and Zucchini

4lb 8oz mussels, cleaned and debearded

1 red onion, finely diced

2 tablespoons olive oil

2 cloves of garlic, finely sliced

½–1 teaspoon red pepper flakes

3½fl oz/⅓ cup dry white wine, or water, as you like

6 jarred piquillo peppers

1 x 14oz can of plum tomatoes, drained of juice and roughly chopped

1 large zucchini, cut into ¾-inch dice

salt and freshly ground black pepper

a small bunch of fresh flat-leaf parsley, leaves finely chopped

juice of ½ a lemon

2 tablespoons salted capers (or use pickled capers), rinsed, drained and roughly chopped

Use canned tomatoes, drained of their juice (keep it for another dish), or chop ripe fresh tomatoes. Jarred piquillo peppers are easy enough to find in most supermarkets nowadays. Slippery and sweet-tasting, they are a bright, handy ingredient to have on your shelves—use them in recipes that call for peppers or in harissa (see page 256). Together with capers and red pepper flakes, this recipe for mussels does a fine job of raiding the pantry.

Prepare the mussels by removing the beards, washing well in cold water and checking they are all tightly closed. Discard any that don't close when tapped on a surface or that have cracked or broken shells.

Fry the onion in a wide-lidded pan over a moderate heat with the olive oil until soft and translucent, about 8–10 minutes. Add the garlic and red pepper flakes and cook for 1 minute. Add the white wine and reduce until all but a tablespoon or so of the liquid remains.

Add the piquillo peppers and the chopped tomatoes and cook until the mixture has thickened and any liquid from the tomatoes has nearly all cooked away.

Add the mussels and diced zucchini to the pan and cover with a lid. Cook over a high heat for about 3 minutes, until all the mussels have opened and are cooked and the zucchini is just tender. Discard any mussels that have refused to open. Check the seasoning of the dish, adding a little salt and plenty of black pepper to taste.

Remove from the heat and add the chopped parsley, a good squeeze of lemon juice and the capers. Serve immediately.

1 whole bulb of garlic, cloves separated and peeled

milk—enough to cover the garlic cloves in a small pan

1 x 2oz can of anchovies in oil, best quality

9oz/1½ cups unsalted butter, cut into ¾-inch dice

9fl oz/1 cup extra virgin olive oil

Bagna Cauda

Cue fanfare—if ever there was a dish more synonymous with conviviality I'm not sure I know of it. You can buy a special bagna cauda dish—a ceramic bowl suspended over a small candle to keep the bagna cauda warm; a bowl set over hot water will work well enough. Share this with friends as an intimate first course. Arrange around it any number of celery sticks, carrots, lettuce leaves, green onions, radishes, cauliflower florets or bell peppers and cooked asparagus, green beans, broccoli and crusty bread for dipping.

Put the garlic cloves into a small pan, cover with milk and simmer for 10 minutes, until the garlic is soft and completely tender. Discard the milk.

Mash the still warm garlic with the anchovies to a paste in a bowl, then scoop the mix into a small clean saucepan with quarter of the butter and put on the lowest heat possible.

As soon as the butter starts to melt, start to whisk the contents of the pan with a small whisk. When the butter is nearly all melted, add the rest bit by bit, still whisking, and continue until all the butter is incorporated. Don't let the pan get too hot—taking it off the heat every now and then is good practice.

Continuing whisking, begin pouring the olive oil very gradually into the still warm mixture until you have a thick, glossy bagna cauda. Remove to a warmed bowl, and serve immediately.

Linguine con Vongole

Verbatim. I am sure lemon and tomato feature well enough in other versions. Here, just clams cooked with olive oil, garlic, chili and white wine, together with pasta, salt, parsley and more olive oil. This is vongole lore—no butter, no lemons, no extra anything—as cooked in Naples by the grandmother who, though she doesn't know it, inspired me to cook.

1lb 2oz small clams, rinsed in cold water

12oz linguine, or use spaghetti

4–5 tablespoons olive oil

3 fat cloves of garlic, finely chopped

½–1 teaspoon red pepper flakes, or finely chopped fresh chili, to taste

3½fl oz/⅓ cup dry white wine, or use vermouth

a small bunch of fresh flat-leaf parsley, leaves finely chopped

SERVES 2

Wash the clams in plenty of cold water, discarding any that don't close when tapped on a surface or that have cracked or broken shells.

Cook the pasta as per the packet instructions, aiming for al dente, then drain, reserving a little of the pasta cooking water in case you should need it to loosen the finished pasta dish.

While the pasta is cooking, put the olive oil into a large pan over a medium heat and add the garlic for 2 minutes, or until it is aromatic but does not brown. Add the chili to the pan in the last 30 or so seconds of cooking time.

Stir the clams and white wine into the garlic pan, then put a lid on the pan and turn up the heat. Cook until the clams open up. As they open, remove those quick to open in batches, reserving them in a bowl and continuing to cook any of the clams that are more stubborn. Continue until all the clams have cooked and released their juices into the saucepan. Discard any clams that refuse to open.

Add the cooked drained spaghetti to the pan and return any clams that you've reserved. Toss well and leave for about 30 seconds to absorb any liquid. Add a little of the reserved pasta cooking liquid should you need it.

Remove from the heat and stir in the chopped parsley. Season with additional salt, more chili and a little more olive oil if necessary. Serve immediately.

1 onion, finely diced

6 cloves of garlic, finely chopped

3 tablespoons olive oil

2 teaspoons sweet paprika

4 tomatoes, peeled and finely chopped, or use canned tomatoes, drained of juice

3½fl oz/⅓ cup white wine

25fl oz/3¼ cups fish stock (see right), or water

salt and freshly ground black pepper

9oz/about 2¼ cups paella rice

20 raw shrimp, peeled and deveined

1lb 12oz of a variety of fresh fish fillets, such as sea bream, sea bass, monkfish, coley (any inexpensive white fish in good supply is fine to use), cut into 1¼-inch pieces—ask for the bones to make the stock!

a small bunch of fresh flat-leaf parsley, leaves finely chopped

lemon wedges, to serve

FOR THE AÏOLI

1 egg yolk

2 cloves of garlic, crushed to a paste

1 teaspoon Dijon mustard

approx. 3½fl oz/⅓ cup olive oil

salt and freshly ground black pepper, to taste

lemon juice, to taste, a good squeeze at the very least

Caldero Fish Soup with Rice and Aïoli

A traditional Spanish fishermen's recipe made on the beach with any fish too inferior to sell at the market, the name of the dish references the small cauldron, a caldero, used to cook this soupy fish and rice dish. Paella rice is crucial, swelling in the stock but still retaining a chewy bite. Aïoli is a good addition to the finished caldero, all pungent and garlicky.

To make a quick fish stock, put about 14oz of fish bones into a saucepan with a peeled clove of garlic, a few fennel and coriander seeds and a few slices of celery and onion. Top up with 1½ pints/3½ cups of water, then bring to the boil, skimming off any froth that collects. Simmer for about 10 minutes, then strain and put to one side until ready to use.

To make the aïoli, place the egg yolk, garlic and mustard in a small bowl and beat together.

Slowly add the olive oil in a steady stream, whisking vigorously all the time until it thickens, adding salt, pepper and lemon juice to taste.

Fry the onion and garlic in the olive oil over a moderate heat until soft and translucent, about 8–10 minutes. Add the paprika and cook for 2 minutes more, then add the tomatoes and cook for 5 minutes.

Add the white wine and fish stock (use water if you like) and bring to the boil, adding salt to taste.

Add the rice and cook for about 20 minutes, or until tender. About 10 minutes before the rice is ready, add the shrimp and the fish. Caldero is supposed to be a little soupy, so add a bit more water if it gets too thick.

When the rice and fish are cooked, add the parsley and serve immediately, with the lemon wedges and aïoli at the table.

Mackerel Recheado

Recheado is a spicy, tangy paste used to stuff and baste fish before shallow frying. You can grill or barbecue the marinated fish if you prefer. Intense in flavor, you want the blend to be thick enough to cling to the fish as you marinate it—the consistency of toothpaste. Tamarind pulp is a brilliant ingredient to have on your shelf. Break off as much as you need and loosen it in a little hot water, pushing the softened pulp through a sieve with the back of a spoon to extract any seeds. Use ready-made tamarind paste, bought in a jar, if you can't find the pulp. Serve the recheado with plain rice and chopped salad—tomatoes, red onion/shallot and cucumber is good. You can use any small to medium whole fish or firm fillets of fish.

Soak the spices, ginger, garlic, ½ teaspoon of salt and the tamarind pulp in the vinegar and sugar for 30 minutes. Then blend until smooth, adding a splash of water if required but ensuring that the paste is thick enough to stick to the fish.

Season the fish with a pinch of salt and stuff the paste right into the slashes, then coat the entire fish with the paste. Marinate for 30 minutes.

You can cook the fish a few ways . . . To fry, heat a ½-inch depth of oil in a large non-stick frying pan. When the oil is shimmering hot, add the whole fish and shallow fry until golden brown on both sides and cooked through—about 2–3 minutes on each side, depending on the thickness of the fish. Alternatively, to grill, heat a grill or barbecue to high and grill the fish for about 3–4 minutes on each side, until cooked through and charred on both sides.

Remove from the heat and serve with lime wedges, with rice and a chopped salad on the side.

1 teaspoon cracked black pepper

1 teaspoon cumin, toasted and ground

½ teaspoon ground turmeric

½ teaspoon ground cinnamon

a pinch of ground cloves (optional)

a pinch of ground cardamom (optional)

2 teaspoons red pepper flakes—more if you like it hotter (you can use fresh chili too)

1 inch fresh ginger, grated or finely sliced

5 cloves of garlic, peeled and chopped in half

salt

3 tablespoons tamarind pulp or paste

3 tablespoons vinegar

1 tablespoon caster sugar

4 mackerel, gutted, well rinsed, dried and slashed to the bone 3 times on each side

neutral oil, for shallow frying

lime wedges, to serve

Sardines with Preserved Lemon and Chili Sauce

Preserved lemons have an intense, salty, citrus flavor. Make your own (see page 284) or use shop-bought. Here used with red chili for a bold sauce, this combination works beautifully with fried or barbecued oily fish. Use mackerel, if you prefer.

5½oz fresh red chilies, long ones not the short round ones, sliced in half and seeds removed

5 cloves of garlic, crushed

1 inch fresh ginger, grated

1 small onion, roughly chopped

3 tablespoons vegetable oil, plus extra for the jar

½–1 or 2 preserved lemons (see page 284), depending on size (unprepared about equal in weight to the quantity of chili), cleaned of their pulp and skin finely chopped

salt and freshly ground black pepper

12 sardines, butterflied or filleted—ask your fishmonger to do this for you

vegetable oil

Blend the chilies, garlic, ginger and onion to a coarse purée in a food processor.

Fry the chili purée in 2 tablespoons of the oil for 5 minutes, until thickened and fragrant, then remove from the heat and stir in the preserved lemon.

Season to taste with salt, about ½–1 teaspoon. If not using the sauce straight away, spoon it into a clean sterilized jar, top with a spoonful of oil to exclude the air from the surface of the sauce, and set aside to cool. Stored in the refrigerator, the sauce will keep for a couple of weeks or so.

Gently rub the sardines all over with a little vegetable oil and season with salt and pepper.

Fry, grill or barbecue the sardines over a moderate to high heat until cooked through, and serve with the preserved lemon and chili sauce on the side.

4 firm white fish fillets, approx.
6oz each—bream, sea bass or grey
mullet, or 16 good-sized shrimp,
peeled and deveined

1-2 fresh red chilies, chopped or
finely sliced

2 cloves of garlic, chopped or
sliced finely

a small bunch of fresh cilantro,
stalks and leaves separated, stalks
finely chopped, leaves roughly
chopped

2 inches fresh ginger, grated or
very finely sliced

grated zest and juice of 1 lime

4 tablespoons grated coconut
(fresh or creamed block)

4 teaspoons coconut oil or neutral
cooking oil

salt

TO SERVE
mashed avocado, chopped
tomatoes, sliced green lettuce,
limes (juice saved) and warm soft
flour tortillas

Coconut Fish Tacos

Cook the parcels of fish in the oven or on the outdoor grill. Have the mashed avocado, chopped tomatoes, lettuce, cilantro leaves and limes ready at the table. Wrap the tortillas in foil and warm them in the oven or on the grill for a minute or two. Bring the parcels to the table and have everyone assemble their own tacos according to taste. I never worry about the fish cooling down once at the table—this is bright summer eating for hot days and warm nights, and nothing needs to be scalding hot.

Preheat the oven to 400°F/gas mark 6.

Assemble the parcels. Cut 4 pieces of foil, each big enough to house a fish fillet. Place the fish fillets skin side down on the foil. Evenly distribute the chilies, garlic, cilantro stalks, ginger, lime zest and coconut between the fillets and add a spoonful of oil and a little salt to each one. Loosely enclose the fish in the foil, sealing all sides but making sure the pouch has enough room for heat to circulate over the fish while cooking.

Space the four foil parcels on a baking tray and place in the hot oven. Cooking time will depend on the size of the fillets. Cook for 6 minutes, then open up the parcels and check to see if the fish is opaque and hot to touch. Remove when it is. If it isn't, reseal and return to the oven to continue cooking.

Remove from the oven and open up the parcels, taking care to not spill any of the cooking juices. Spoon the juices back over the fish and squeeze over the lime juice.

To assemble the tacos, place some mashed avocado, chopped tomatoes, shredded lettuce, reserved cilantro leaves and more chili, if you like, on each of the warm tortillas and distribute the cooked fish between them, spooning over some of the cooking juices.

Roll up the tortillas and serve.

9 SWEET STUFF

I have a love-hate relationship with desserts. Given a choice, I will always opt to cook and eat something savory over something sweet. In a restaurant, I will always choose good cheese over dessert. I am first in line to bring a main course offering to any friend's potluck suppers—I rarely bring dessert. I like sweet things but hardly ever make them. And yet, I am aware that to be able to effortlessly offer something sweet at the end of a meal is always a good thing.

Setting the scene: I think it must have been about my third or fourth job as a chef in London. It was in a restaurant I had really wanted to work in. The restaurant had a gorgeous leafy garden near the Thames (good for sunbathing on split shifts), a quirky roster that gave you every other weekend off (the holy grail in restaurant life), good produce and relative freedom with what you could do with it menu-wise. On the day of the interview (I say interview, but there I stood in the kitchen surrounded by bubbling pots and the chefs all listening keenly) I lied and told the owner I had experience in pastry and would be willing to cover that position in the kitchen. In what was then my short career as a chef, what I loved most about learning to cook professionally was developing my taste, discovering different ingredients and mastering new cooking techniques and skills. I reveled under the intense pressure of cooking in a team for big numbers, of sending food out on time and in unison to the other chefs in the kitchen. How, when you are really flying on a restaurant service, you begin to feel an innate connection with what you are cooking, adjusting and tinkering with numerous different items in the same moment, and on cue sending out finished dishes to waiting customers.

Pastry or pâtisserie work is a very different kitchen discipline. As a pastry chef you have to be far more exacting with your cooking; for more finicky recipes you have to follow them to the letter. It is a craft, a science of sorts. There is less space for culinary spontaneity, less room to maneuver within a recipe. In a small restaurant team, the pastry chef will often work alone and at a different kilter to the rest of the kitchen. If you don't count the very smart restaurants serving flash canapés, pastry chefs are last off the blocks on a service and last out of the kitchen at the end of the day. As for me, I hated it. I didn't enjoy the lonesome and nerve-racking accuracy of pastry work and far preferred the nuance of cooking in tandem at the stoves with the other chefs in the kitchen. It wasn't long, a week at most, before the chef on the hot (stove) section (we shared an oven in prep time) queried my pastry credentials. I can barely remember my litany of pastry fails from that week, I think I've blocked them out, but a leaking lemon tart finally gave the game away. I confessed to the curious chef, who then offered to switch positions in the kitchen with me. He felt like a change, he said, and was sure the owner wouldn't mind. His name was Matthew, and I later married him.

In the years following my failed stint as a pastry chef, and the many kitchens I have worked in since, I have managed to carve out an approach to desserts and pastry work that I am proud of. I have come to realize that the puddings and desserts I love to make the most, no surprises here, are often the simplest ones. For example, I love bottling fruit and find it gives way to a sort of beautiful patience, when you have ripe seasonal fruit and capture it at its most perfect, suspending it in flavorful syrup. Stored in the refrigerator, bottled fruits will last for up to a month or more and give you an elegant dessert matched with a little cream, ice cream or thick Greek yogurt. With the fruit long gone, you can then freeze the fragrant syrup in molds for knockout ice lollies (see page 282), dilute with sparkling water and lots of ice for a refreshing long drink, or use short measures of the syrup in any cocktail-making. Quick freezes like the chocolate and prune juice sorbet (see page 298) or the honey, pear and bay leaf ice cream (see page 296) have so few ingredients, they are as stark as they are delicious.

Most prominent in my pantry and in sweet cooking, not least in my first cup of morning tea or spread on the children's toast, is honey. I am lucky that my stepfather has some beehives in the field behind his house. I love how the character of the honey changes with the season as the various flowers in the fields come into blossom. The first of the season's honey is grassy, quickly turning almost fudgy in consistency; the bees have mostly fed on rapeseed flowers. Later on in the summer, when the meadows are flush with a variety of colorful wildflowers, if it has been a good year and the bees have fed well, they will produce yet more honeycomb still, and their honey is softer and more floral in taste. In the honey, nutmeg and black tea bread (see recipe 286) or spooned over grilled cinnamon oranges, the extraordinary complexity of honey is alchemy in these disarmingly simple recipes.

You'll find my enthusiasm for good stale bread does not stop at desserts, and the banana pain perdu (see page 288) and caramelized apple and maple bread pudding (see page 290) are both flattered by the addition of robust cooked-again bread. As for brown bread? Everyone knows that brown bread ice cream really is the very best sort of ice cream, and I make mine with rye bread and include malt extract for a nutty flavor (see page 294). Where I can relish the slow pace of baking with sourdough, the lure of setting about a shop-bought panettone, slicing it open and filling it with a ludicrously easy-to-make Sicilian-style cassata filling (see page 287) is a telling comparison and says a lot about my approach to desserts. Bursting at the seams with ricotta, nuts, and dried fruit, I honestly cannot imagine a more impressive, or more colossal dessert to serve as a special dessert.

With more recipes in this chapter than I can draw your attention to individually, read on for my blueprint on all things sweet. To close, what I will say is that I can't get enough of rose water (never the strong essence), splashed here and there in bottled fruit syrups, for example, and especially when matched with soft berry fruit and cream, as in the blackberry, rose water and pistachio freezer cake (see page 304). I love its dusty ethereal whiff and buy rose water often from my local Turkish shop, a clear bottle with a gaudy display of pink roses on the label. In addition, stem ginger, cocoa, treacle, molasses, condensed milk, candied peel, dried fruit and nuts—these ingredients sit together on my shelf and I value the year-round reliability they offer to my cooking. And finally, a few squares of deep dark chocolate, high in cocoa solids, is the very best dessert of all, and I always have a bar or two in my pantry.

PANTRY BASICS

bottled fruit (see pages 280–3)

honey

condensed milk

molasses

maple syrup

cocoa powder

dark chocolate
(70 per cent cocoa solids)

whole almonds

ground almonds

hazelnuts

pistachio nuts

unsalted peanuts

peanut butter

candied peel

raisins

dried dates

dried figs

rose water

stem ginger

walnuts

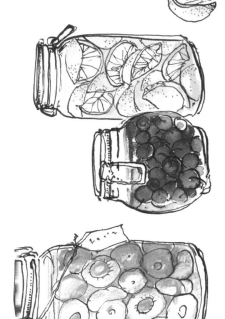

HOW TO BOTTLE FRUIT
FOR THE REFRIGERATOR

Fruit for bottling should be ripe, but firm, and never over-ripe or bruised. Small fruits may be left whole, but larger fruits with pits should be halved or quartered. Apples and pears are good bottled, though they should be first peeled and also cored. To peel fruit with a skin, peaches or apricots for example, briefly blanch the whole fruits in plenty of boiling water until the skin loosens—about 3–5 minutes—then drain and cool in a bowl of cold water with some ice cubes in it. The skin should slip off easily.

Syrup preserves the longevity of the fruit in terms of color, taste and texture. The syrup will also eventually take on the flavor and color of the fruit. To make syrups, slowly bring cold water and sugar to boiling point and simmer until the sugar has dissolved; 10½oz/1½ cups of sugar to 17fl oz/2 cups of water is a good ratio to use and will make about 27fl oz/3½ cups of syrup. This should easily be enough for a large punnet of soft fruit or 6 or so peaches, for example, depending on the size of the fruit you are bottling and the jar you are using. You can use wine instead of water if you like, diluted or straight. You can flavor the syrup with any number of additional ingredients. Choose ingredients that will flatter the fruit you are bottling. Vanilla pods, bay leaves, allspice, star anise, cinnamon quills, juniper, clove, citrus peel, fresh ginger, kaffir lime leaves, lavender buds, rose water or petals, orange flower water, peppercorns, red pepper flakes, thyme, mace blades, cardamoms and elderflower heads are all wonderful when paired in simpatico groups and bottled with complementary fruits.

The ice lolly opposite is a sensational combination. It's simply the frozen syrup from some bottled peaches, including kaffir lime leaves, cloves, cinnamon and star anise. The cherries pictured on page 1 were bottled simply in sugar syrup with star anise and a few peppercorns.

Fruit may be bottled cooked or raw, depending on the type you choose to use. Bottled raw is best for soft fruits such as berries, plums, currants and cherries. Firm fruits such as apples and pears are best cooked in the sugar syrup until soft, making them more manageable to pack into jars. Cook peeled pitted fruit in the syrup until just tender—pierceable with a thin skewer. Add lemon juice or a splash of white wine vinegar to any syrup destined to bottle fruit that will oxidize; apples and pears for example.

Jars must be sterilized well before use. Wash any jars in clean, hot, soapy water, rinse well, then stand the washed jars upside down in the oven at 300°F/gas mark 2 for 25–30 minutes. The jars should be hot when you ladle in the hot fruit and the hot syrup.

Pack the fruit into the jars in layers, ladling hot syrup over each layer as you do so. Firmly tap the jars on the work surface to remove any bubbles before putting the lids on tightly. Cool down, then store in the refrigerator. The bottled fruit will keep for a month or more if refrigerated.

Preserved Oranges and Lemons

Intensely citrusy with a sharp, salty burst, preserved oranges and lemons are a wonderful seasoning to have in your pantry. Chop with dill, parsley and pine nuts for a pesto to serve with vegetables (see page 218), blend with fresh chili for a sauce to serve with fish (see page 270), or chop fine and stir through cooked grains—pilaf, for example.

6–8 unwaxed oranges or lemons (use blood or Seville oranges if you like)

approx. 1 tablespoon coarse sea salt per fruit

NOTE

To use preserved lemons and oranges, remove the required amount of fruit from the jar, rinse under cold running water and pat dry. Split the fruit in half, then scrape out and discard the pulp. Slice the preserved peel into thin strips or cut into small dice for use.

Wash and sterilize a 17fl oz Kilner jar (see page 283).

Wash the fruit under running water and dry. If the fruit is waxed, wash it under hot running water and scrub it firmly with a clean wire brush.

Cut each fruit almost in half vertically, then alomst halve it again, making an X shape down the fruit but keeping the base intact.

Spoon about 1 tablespoon of coarse salt into a cut orange or lemon and place the salt-filled fruit in the sterilized jar.

Continue until you have prepared all the fruit and filled the jar with the salted fruit. Press the fruit down firmly in the jar to extract some of the juice. Put the lid on the jar and leave for a few hours or overnight.

Press the fruit down firmly again, extracting more juice. The fruit will have started to soften.

Leave the jar somewhere cool and dark for at least 4 weeks. Turn the jar upside down every couple of days or so. If the top fruits in the jar remain exposed, add more orange or lemon juice to top the level up.

Once the fruits are completely soft, they are ready to use. Once opened, you must store the fruit in the refrigerator. It will keep for upwards of a year.

Honey, Nutmeg and Black Tea Bread

8oz/1¾ cups all-purpose flour

¼ of a nutmeg, freshly grated

3½oz/½ cup soft brown sugar

a pinch of salt

1 teaspoon baking powder

1 teaspoon baking soda

3½oz/about ⅜ cup honey

5fl oz/⅔ cup hot black tea

MAKES 8–10 SLICES

Preheat the oven to 325°F/gas mark 3. Grease a 1lb loaf tin and line it with baking parchment.

Mix the flour, nutmeg, sugar, salt, baking powder and baking soda together in a large bowl.

Melt the honey in the hot tea in a separate mixing bowl. Mix well to dissolve the honey. Pour the wet mixture into the dry ingredients and mix well.

Spoon the mixture into the prepared tin and bake in the oven for 35–40 minutes, until a skewer comes out clean when inserted into the center of the cake.

Remove from the tin and allow to cool before slicing.

Nut Butter

Making your own nut butter is addictive. Simply, nuts blitzed to form butter. Experiment with using different nuts.

1lb 2oz/3¾ cups roasted unsalted peanuts, or use other nuts

1 tablespoon coconut or vegetable oil

¼–½ teaspoon salt, or to taste

approx. 1–2 teaspoons honey or sugar, or to taste (optional)

MAKES 1LB 2OZ/2½ CUPS

Place three-quarters of the nuts, the oil and the salt in the bowl of a food processor and process until the nuts break down, stopping occasionally to scrape the sides of the bowl as needed.

Continue to process until the peanut butter is smooth, then add the remaining nuts and the honey or sugar if using, and process until it reaches the texture you like, crunchy or smooth.

Transfer to a clean jar with a lid and put into the refrigerator to chill. Stored covered in the refrigerator, the nut butter will keep for up to 2 weeks.

Panettone Stuffed Full with Cassata

One panettone, filled, will easily feed 8 people. This cake will eat just as beautifully the next day. It is incredibly rich, so any leftovers are a boon.

1lb 2oz/2½ cups ricotta

4oz/¾ cup confectioners' sugar (reserve 1 tablespoon to dust)

3½oz/about ¾ cup pistachios, almonds or hazelnuts, finely chopped

3½oz/about ¾ cup mixture of at least 3 of the following: dried cherries, cranberries, raisins, currants, chopped figs or candied peel

3oz/about ½ cup coarsely grated dark chocolate,

1 x approx. 2lb 4oz panettone

3½fl oz/⅓ cup Marsala wine, or use sweet sherry or Moscato wine

Line a bowl (roughly the same size as the panettone) with two layers of overlapping plastic wrap, making sure you have a wide measure of plastic wrap hanging over the sides of the bowl.

Mix the ricotta with the confectioners' sugar, nuts, dried fruit and grated chocolate and set to one side.

Cut off the top of the panettone, about ¾ inch thick is good, and place the slice cut side up at the bottom of the plastic wrap-lined bowl. Drizzle with a splash of the Marsala wine. Cut a further two ¾ inch thick disks off the panettone and put to one side to use as further layers.

Slice the remaining panettone in vertical slices down the shape of the cake, giving you wide slices of cake. Drizzle these slices with some of the Marsala wine. Position these slices snugly around the sides of the bowl, forming the encasing wall of the dessert.

Add half the ricotta mix to the hollow-shaped panettone mould. Gently flatten the mix out with a spoon, then place one of the reserved disks of panettone on top and drizzle with a bit more Marsala. Spoon the remaining ricotta mix on top of the disk and add the final disk of panettone to form the top or lid of the cake. Drizzle with the last of the Marsala.

Fold the overlapping plastic wrap securely over the top of the molded panettone cake shape and weight it down with a plate and a few cans from the pantry.

Refrigerate overnight, or for a few hours at least.

When ready to serve, peel back the plastic wrap and turn the cake upside down on to a serving plate. Remove the remaining plastic wrap and sift a little confectioners' sugar over the top before serving.

Banana Pain Perdu with Cardamom and Buttermilk

Pain perdu, or lost bread, is a tremendous way to use up any stale bread. Softened here in a mixture of buttermilk and banana with cardamom, it is an easy and quirky interpretation of banana bread.

1 large, very ripe speckled banana

10fl oz/1¼ cups buttermilk (use yogurt thinned with milk if you prefer)

1 egg

a pinch of salt

approx. ¼ teaspoon ground cardamom (or use the quatre épices on page 163)

a pinch of ground cinnamon, to taste

a splash of milk (optional)

4 slices of good-quality stale bread

butter, for frying

TO SERVE

runny honey, maple syrup, toasted nuts, seeds, more banana, as you like

Mash the banana in a large shallow bowl and whisk in the buttermilk, egg, salt and spices. If the batter appears too thick (it should be pourable), add a splash of milk to thin it out.

Let the batter rest for 5 minutes and preheat a non-stick frying pan.

Dip the bread slices into the batter and let the bread absorb some of the mixture for a few seconds on each side.

Add a knob of butter to the frying pan and swirl to coat. Over a moderate heat, add the soaked bread and cook for about 2–3 minutes each side, until golden brown.

Serve immediately.

3/4oz/just over 1 tablespoon butter, diced

8 slices of day-or-two-old stale bread, crusts removed and cut into 1¼-inch cubes

5½oz/¾ cup brown sugar

2 large apples, peeled and diced into small pieces

4 eggs

10fl oz/1¼ cups full fat milk

10fl oz/1¼ cups heavy cream

3½fl oz/⅓ cup maple syrup

a pinch of salt

3 teaspoons quatre épices (see page 163)

heavy cream or yogurt, to serve (optional)

SERVES 4–6

Caramelized Apple and Maple Bread Pudding

Preheat the oven to 350°F/gas mark 4. Grease a baking dish with half the butter.

In a large mixing bowl, toss together the bread cubes, brown sugar and apple pieces. Transfer to the baking dish and roast in the hot oven for 15 minutes. Remove from the oven and set to one side.

Using the same mixing bowl, whisk together the rest of the ingredients apart from the remaining butter. Pour over the bread/apple mixture in the baking dish and gently combine, making sure each piece of bread is soaked in the egg and milk mixture. Let it stand for 10 minutes.

When the egg/milk mixture has mostly soaked into the bread, dab the remaining butter all over the bread-and-apple-soaked mix, then place the baking dish in the preheated oven and bake for 40–50 minutes, or until the centre is set and the top is nice and golden.

Remove from the oven and rest for 5 minutes before serving with heavy cream or yogurt.

Oranges Grilled with Honey and Cinnamon with Ricotta and Amaretti

A super-easy and beautiful dessert—works equally well with grilled apricots or peaches.

4 oranges, peeled and cut into thick slices

approx. 3 tablespoons runny honey

2 teaspoons ground cinnamon

2¾oz/about ½ cup amaretti biscuits, crushed

7oz/1 cup ricotta

Line a baking tray with foil and preheat the grill.

Add the orange slices to the tray and drizzle with honey to taste. Add the cinnamon.

Grill under the hot grill until the honey is bubbling and some of the oranges have begun to caramelize a little—about 10 minutes. Remove from the grill and set to one side for about 5 minutes. Arrange the slices on a serving plate.

Roughly smash the amaretti biscuits and arrange blobs of ricotta and the broken amaretti over the grilled oranges. Drizzle over a little extra honey and serve.

Brown Bread and Malt
Ice Cream

3oz/about ⅓ cup brown sugar

2 thick slices of brown bread (or use 2 small brown rolls) pulsed in a food processor to make a fine crumb

1 tablespoon malt extract

10fl oz/1¼ cups heavy cream

3 oz/about ⅔ cup confectioners' sugar, sifted (or use superfine sugar)

2 eggs, separated

MAKES JUST UNDER 17FL OZ

Preheat the oven to 400°F/gas mark 6.

Combine the brown sugar with the breadcrumbs and spread thinly on a baking tray. Dribble over the malt extract.

Roast for 15–20 minutes, stirring frequently, until caramelized and crunchy. Remove from the oven and leave to cool.

Whisk the cream with half the confectioners' sugar until soft peaks form. Do not over-beat it.

Beat the remaining confectioners' sugar with the egg yolks until pale and fluffy, using an electric whisk.

In a clean, dry mixing bowl, whisk the egg whites until stiff.

In a large mixing bowl, gently combine the three whipped mixtures together—the cream, egg yolk and egg white. Gently stir in the cold caramelized breadcrumbs (they may need breaking up a little if they have clumped together).

Pour into a container and freeze for at least 4 hours. The ice cream may need to be softened slightly in the refrigerator for 15 minutes before serving.

Coconut Kulfi

Just four ingredients here—these are the perfect end to a spicy, fiery meal.

1 x 14fl oz can of coconut milk (whisked together if it has separated)

3 cardamom pods, slightly crushed

7oz/½ cup sweetened condensed milk

1½oz/about ½ cup desiccated coconut

MAKES 4–6, DEPENDING ON SIZE OF MOLD

Bring half the coconut milk to the boil with the cardamoms. Remove from the heat and let it infuse for 10 minutes. Strain and leave to cool.

Stir in the remaining coconut milk and the condensed milk.

Pour the mix into ice lolly molds (conical shapes are traditional) and freeze until completely solid, which should take about 3 hours.

When they are ready to eat, toast the coconut in a dry pan over a moderate heat until golden, then remove from the heat and leave to cool.

Pop the kulfi out of the moulds by holding each mould briefly under running hot water, and put them up-ended on a serving plate. Scatter each with some of the cooled toasted coconut to serve.

1lb 5oz ripe pears, peeled, cored
and chopped small

2 or 3 bay leaves, torn in half

5½oz/about ½ cup runny honey

10fl oz/1¼ cups heavy cream

3½fl oz/⅓ cup full fat milk

MAKES APPROX. 27FL OZ

Honey, Bay and Pear
Ice Cream

In a covered saucepan over a moderate heat, cover
and cook the pears together with the bay leaves and a
splash of water (about 1fl oz/2 tablespoons) until they
are completely soft. Remove from the heat and add the
honey, stirring to melt.

Remove the bay leaves and blend the pears until
smooth. Chill in the refrigerator until cold.

Stir in the cream and milk and churn in an ice-cream
machine, then freeze for at least 3 hours.

If you don't have an ice cream machine, use just the
cream, whipping to soft peaks and gently folding in the
soft pears and honey before freezing.

19fl oz/2⅓ cups prune juice

7oz/1 cup sugar

1¾oz/just under ½ cup unsweetened good-quality cocoa powder

a pinch of salt

5½oz/1 cup finely chopped bittersweet or semi-sweet chocolate

½ teaspoon vanilla extract

chilled cream, to serve

MAKES APPROX. 1½ PINTS

Prune Juice and Chocolate Sorbet

This is very rich; one small scoop per person is enough. Some cold cream dribbled over the sorbet is delicious.

Whisk half the prune juice with the sugar, cocoa and salt. Put into a large saucepan and whisk while the mixture comes to the boil, then simmer gently for 1 minute.

Remove from the heat, add the chocolate and stir until it's all melted, then add the remaining prune juice.

Transfer to a blender and blend the mix for 15 seconds.

Chill thoroughly, then churn in an ice cream machine according to the manufacturer's instructions.

Walnut and Date and Sunflower Seed Bars

The sticky layer of date purée in the middle of these flapjacks makes them something very special.

1lb/about 3 cups pitted dates (or use dried figs)

4 tablespoons coconut or sunflower oil, plus extra to grease

12oz/about 3½ cups oats

3½oz/¾ cup sunflower seeds

a pinch of salt

2 teaspoons ground cinnamon, or use quatre épices (see page 163)

3½oz/¾ cup walnuts, roughly chopped

MAKES APPROX. 16 BARS, DEPENDING ON SIZE

Preheat the oven to 375°F/gas mark 5.

Blend the dates to a smooth purée with the oil and 12fl oz/1½ cups of water.

Mix three-quarters of the date purée with the oats, sunflower seeds, salt and spice in a mixing bowl.

Line a baking tray, about 9 x 9 inches, with baking parchment and grease it with some extra oil or butter. Pour half the oat mix into the tray and spread it out evenly. Spread the rest of the date purée over the top of the oat mixture and cover with the last of the oat mix. Top with the chopped walnuts.

Bake in the oven for about 20–30 minutes, until the oats turn golden and the nuts are nicely roasted.

Remove from the oven and leave to cool for about 20 minutes before cutting into bars.

Portuguese Molasses Cake

7oz/1½ cups mixed dried fruit (use a bought combination or use any or all of the following: raisins, currants, chopped dried figs, chopped dried dates or chopped dried cherries)

¼oz sachet of dried yeast

3½fl oz/⅓ cup Madeira, or use port

4½oz skinned walnuts or almonds (or buy them ready-chopped and don't pulse)

1lb 2oz/3¾ cups all-purpose flour

1 level teaspoon salt

1 teaspoon baking soda

1 teaspoon ground ginger, or use ground star anise

¼–½ nutmeg, freshly grated

1 teaspoon ground cinnamon

¼ teaspoon ground cloves, or use 2–3 teaspoons quatre épices (see page 163) instead of the above four if you have some made up that wants using

12oz/1¾ cups unsalted butter, softened, plus extra for greasing tin

7oz/1 cup sugar

4 eggs

14oz/about 1 cup molasses (or use runny honey)

MAKES 1 × 9 INCH CAKE

A Portuguese wine importer friend brought this impressive cake along to a tasting. Served with Madeira, the combination of spiced, treacly cake and the wine was mind-blowing. Lard is sometimes used in lieu of some of the butter; I'll leave this up to you. Molasses lends depth of flavor and the spices give aromatic complexity. You can alter the balance of spice if you like, adding more of each for a spicier cake – just go easy on the clove, as your palate will be numbed.

Soak the dried fruit and yeast in the Madeira or port for at least 30 minutes.

Pulse the nuts in a food processor until coarsely chopped. Put them into a bowl with the flour, salt, baking soda and spices, and mix to combine.

Beat together the butter and sugar in a large bowl using an electric mixer until pale and fluffy. Add the eggs 1 at a time, beating well after each addition.

Add one third of the flour mixture to all of the butter mixture and mix until combined, using a hand mixer at a low speed, then add the molasses and mix well. Add another third of the flour mixture and mix until combined. Add the dried fruit and yeast mixture and the final third of the flour mix. Stir well to combine. Leave the cake mix covered in the mixing bowl for 45 minutes to prove slightly.

Preheat the oven to 325°F/gas mark 3, grease a 9-inch round cake tin or equivalent square tin and line with baking parchment.

Pour and scrape the proved cake mix into the prepared tin and bake on the middle shelf of the oven for approximately 1 hour and 30 minutes, or until a skewer inserted in the center comes out clean. If the top of the cake begins to color too much towards the end of the cooking time, cover with a piece of foil.

Remove from the oven and cool in the tin for 15 minutes, then remove from the tin and cool completely. Wrapped in foil or stored in a cake tin, the cake will keep for up to a week.

9oz/1¼ cups unsalted butter,
chopped into small pieces, plus
extra for greasing

10½oz/2 cups dark chocolate,
chopped into small pieces

2 tablespoons stem ginger syrup

9oz/1½ cups soft brown sugar

5 eggs

3 balls of stem ginger, finely
chopped

MAKES 1 X 9-INCH CAKE

Chocolate and Stem Ginger Flourless Cake

A bit like a soufflé, flourless chocolate cake will puff up in the cooking process, sinking a little as it cools, to give a cake that is both light to eat and deliciously chocolate-y. Chocolate and stem ginger are a wonderful match here.

Heat the oven to 325°F/gas mark 3, grease a 9-inch round springform tin and line with a disk of baking parchment.

Put the chocolate and butter into a medium-sized heatproof bowl, add the ginger syrup and set the bowl over a pan of barely simmering water. Stir occasionally until melted and smooth. Remove from the heat and cool slightly. Use a microwave here if you prefer.

Whisk the sugar and eggs in a large mixing bowl using an electric mixer until pale, light and increased in volume.

Pour the melted chocolate and butter into the eggs and stir until smooth, then finally add the finely chopped ginger.

Spoon the mixture into the prepared tin and gently spread level, using the back of a spoon.

Bake on the middle shelf of the oven for 40–45 minutes, or until lightly crisp on top but slightly gooey on the inside. Leave the cake to cool completely in the tin.

Mexican/Spanish Horchata
Toasted Rice

A traditional Mexican drink made with toasted rice and cinnamon. If you want a thicker drink, add a small handful of toasted blanched almonds (about 1oz/¼ cup), blitz with the rice-infused milk in a blender until smooth, then strain before serving. Horchata can also be made using rice milk for a dairy-free drink.

Toast the rice in a dry pan over a medium heat—it should take about 5 minutes to turn a gentle nutty brown.

Add the cinnamon stick to the rice, then pour the cold milk into the pan over the hot rice and add sugar to taste. Remove from the heat and set to one side to cool completely. Put the mixture into the refrigerator to chill down for at least 6 hours.

To serve, blend the chilled milk-soaked rice, add a little extra water or milk to loosen if desired, then strain and serve in tall glasses with plenty of ice and dusted with cinnamon.

3½oz/½ cup any white rice

1 cinnamon stick

17fl oz/2 cups full fat milk, or use water if you like

3 tablespoons superfine sugar, to taste, or use honey

ice cubes and ground cinnamon, to serve

MAKES 17FL OZ/2 CUPS

Blackberry, Rose Water and Pistachio Freezer Cake

10½oz/2¼ cups blackberries

1¾fl oz/just under ¼ cup pomegranate molasses

12fl oz/1½ cups heavy cream

1–2 teaspoons rose water, to taste

2¾oz/about ⅜ cup sugar

15 lady finger or savoiardi biscuits, chopped into ¾-inch pieces

2¾oz/about ½ cup pistachio purée and sprinkle with a quarter of the pistachios, or use shelled pistachios and roughly chop them

MAKES 1 X 1 LB LOAF TIN

Blend 9oz/about 1¾ cups of the blackberries with the pomegranate molasses to a rough purée.

Whisk the cream with the rose water and sugar until it holds stiff peaks.

Line the bottom of a 1lb loaf tin with plastic wrap. Sprinkle with a quarter of the biscuits. Spread on a quarter of the cream and a quarter of the blackberry purée and sprinkle with a quarter of the pistachios. Repeat for three more layers – run a knife through the loaf tin a couple of times to marble and ripple the layers – and finish with a layer of pistachios.

Cover with plastic wrap and chill in the freezer for at least 3 hours before serving.

Remove from the freezer, turn out on to a plate, pistachio side up, and serve in slices with the remaining blackberries.

Spiced Fig Butter

Serve this for breakfast on thick slices of toast. Salted butter is best, giving flavor to the sweet dried fruit. Use dates if you prefer.

Mash the butter, figs and spice together and chill in the refrigerator for at least 30 minutes before serving.

9oz/1¼ cups salted butter, room temperature

9oz/1⅔ cups dried figs (the softer the better), finely chopped

1 heaped teaspoon mixed spice, or use quatre épices (see page 163)

Marzipan and Roasted Nectarine Cake

I've always hated marzipan served as a thick slice between the Christmas cake and the layer of fondant icing. Chopped small and cooked in a cake batter, however, the marzipan here does something wonderful to the cake crumb, turning fudgy, sweet and unmistakably almondy.

4½oz/½ cup butter, softened, plus extra for greasing

2 eggs, lightly beaten

4½oz/just under ⅔ cup superfine sugar, plus an extra 2 tablespoons to toss and sprinkle

4½oz/1 cup all-purpose flour

1¾oz/½ cup ground almonds

1 teaspoon baking powder

a pinch of salt

3½oz/½ cup plain yogurt

3½oz/about ⅓ cup marzipan, cold, finely chopped

2 ripe nectarines, halved, pitted and sliced

confectioners' sugar, to dust

MAKES 1 X 8½-INCH CAKE

Preheat the oven to 375°F/gas mark 5. Grease an 8½-inch springform cake tin and line with baking parchment.

Put all the ingredients apart from the marzipan, nectarines and confectioners' sugar into a food processor and pulse until smooth. Stir in the marzipan and spoon the batter into the prepared tin.

Toss the nectarine slices with 1 tablespoon sugar and lay them on top of the cake batter.

Sprinkle with 1 more tablespoon of sugar and bake for about 45 minutes, or until a skewer inserted into the middle comes out clean.

Leave the cake to cool in the tin for 10 minutes before removing, then peel off the parchment and slide the cake on to a plate. Dust lightly with confectioners' sugar before serving.

3½oz/½ cup sugar

2 ripe peaches, halved, pitted and thinly sliced

1-2 Earl Grey tea bags (or use 1-2 tablespoons loose tea leaves), depending on how strong you like it (black tea can also be used)

Iced Peach and Earl Grey Tea

The bergamot flavor of Earl Grey tea is gorgeous here with the peach syrup. Serve in tall glasses, with lots of ice and more sliced fresh peach.

Bring 3½fl oz/⅓ cup of water to the boil with the sugar and one of the sliced peaches in a small saucepan, then reduce the heat and simmer until the sugar is dissolved. Remove from the heat and set to one side to infuse for at least an hour or so.

In the meantime, brew the tea for about 4 minutes in 1¾ pints/4 cups of hot water and allow to cool. Strain into a big jug and put into the refrigerator to chill completely.

Strain the cooked peach slices from the syrup (eat them with some Greek yogurt or ice cream) and pop the syrup into the refrigerator to cool.

Add the peach syrup to the tea and serve over ice with the remaining fresh sliced peach.

Laos Iced Coffee

In Laos you can buy iced coffee from street vendors, who sell it in small clear plastic bags clunking with ice, secured at the top with a rubber band and with a straw poking out the top.

In a large jug mix the condensed milk with the coffee, stirring well to melt the condensed milk.

Put lots of ice into each serving glass.

Pour the coffee mix over the ice and serve immediately.

4½oz/just under ¼ cup sweetened condensed milk

3 x 8fl oz cups of hot, strong coffee, or use an espresso measure topped up with boiling water

lots of sturdy ice cubes, at least 4 per serving

Index

ACKNOWLEDGEMENTS

Thank you mostly to Matthew who helped with all the recipes in this book. We're quite a team. Sarah Lavelle, thank you for really stretching me to write the book you knew I wanted to write. Thank you also Diana Henry for your thoughtful support in the infancy of this book. To all my friends; there were those who cooked the book, there were some (my mum included) who whipped the kids off and out so I could write it, and some who rallied a 'you can do it!' cheer nearing deadline when I looked about to burst – massive love and I will, of course, cook for you all any time. Thanks to Mike Lusmore and Stephanie Boote for the relaxed and beautiful photography days, Nick and Juliana Hounsfield for the loan of your gorgeous, light kitchen; it was fun feeding you all. Snow at Bibico, I do love a good dress. Degusta, Bristol, your Spanish produce rocks. Nick Saltmarsh at Hodmedod, thank you for setting me straight on all things fava. Also Annie Lee, who is a dynamo as copy editor. And lastly, my three brilliant children, Grace, Ivy and Dorothy: I love cooking for you and I always will.

THANKS ALSO...

Denby pottery were particularly kind: many thanks for pieces from their various beautiful collections. www.denby.co.uk

Sytch Farm Studios, such beautiful wares. www.sytchfarmstudios.co.uk

Tableware by Rose & Grey. www.roseandgrey.co.uk.

Tableware & Furniture by Loaf. www.loaf.com

Catherine Waters Antiques in Tetbury. @catherinewatersantiques

Marc Giddings for the Wonki Ware

Laura Reynolds at Fifteen Twelve. www.fifteentwelve.co.uk

Publishing Director: Sarah Lavelle
Creative Director: Helen Lewis
Copy Editor: Annie Lee
Editorial Assistant: Harriet Webster
Designer: Nicola Ellis
Photographer: Mike Lusmore
Illustrator: Andy Mosse
Food Stylist: Stephanie Boote
Production: Vincent Smith and Tom Moore

First published in 2017 by
Quadrille Publishing Limited
Pentagon House
52–54 Southwark Street
London SE1 1UN
www.quadrille.com

Quadrille is an imprint of Hardie Grant
www.hardiegrant.com

Text © Claire Thomson 2017
Photography © Mike Lusmore 2017
Illustration © Andy Mosse 2017
Design and layout © Quadrille Publishing Limited 2017

Cataloguing in Publication Data: a catalogue record for this book is available from the British Library.

ISBN: 978 178713 047 0

Printed in China